The Worship Of Mithras And

Serapis

C. W. King

Kessinger Publishing's Rare Reprints

Thousands of Scarce and Hard-to-Find Books on These and other Subjects!

- Americana
- Ancient Mysteries
- Animals
- Anthropology
- Architecture
- Arts
- Astrology
- Bibliographies
- Biographies & Memoirs
- Body, Mind & Spirit
- Business & Investing
- Children & Young Adult
- Collectibles
- Comparative Religions
- Crafts & Hobbies
- Earth Sciences
- Education
- Ephemera
- Fiction
- Folklore
- Geography
- Health & Diet
- History
- Hobbies & Leisure
- Humor
- Illustrated Books
- Language & Culture
- Law
- Life Sciences
- Literature
- Medicine & Pharmacy
- Metaphysical
- Music
- Mystery & Crime
- Mythology
- Natural History
- Outdoor & Nature
- Philosophy
- Poetry
- Political Science
- Science
- Psychiatry & Psychology
- Reference
- Religion & Spiritualism
- Rhetoric
- Sacred Books
- Science Fiction
- Science & Technology
- Self-Help
- Social Sciences
- Symbolism
- Theatre & Drama
- Theology
- Travel & Explorations
- War & Military
- Women
- Yoga
- *Plus Much More!*

We kindly invite you to view our catalog list at:
http://www.kessinger.net

PART II.

THE WORSHIP OF MITHRAS AND SERAPIS.

"O voi ch'avete gl'intelletti sani,
 Mirate la dottrina che s'asconde
 Sotto il velame degli versi strani."

"Salve vera Deûm facies, vultusque paterne,
Octo et sexcentis numeris cui litera trina
Conformat sacrum nomen, cognomen et
Omen. (Mart. Capella. Hymn. ad Sol.)

$$\Phi PH = \mathbf{T}HC = {}_{\llcorner}\mathbf{I}_{\lrcorner} = {}_{\llcorner}\mathbf{X}_{\lrcorner}.$$

THE WORSHIP OF MITHRAS.

I. ORIGIN OF MITHRAICISM.

THE innumerable monuments of every kind bequeathed to us by the widely-spread worship of the deity styled *Mithras*, serve, at the same time, copiously to illustrate the important contributions of Zoroastrian doctrine towards the composition of Gnosticism. The Mithraic religion, according to Plutarch, first made its appearance in Italy upon Pompey's reduction of the Cilician Pirates, of whom it was the national worship; * and who, when broken up into colonists and slaves all over Italy, propagated it amongst their conquerors. In the new soil the novel religion flourished so rapidly as, in the space of two centuries, to supersede (coupled with the earlier introduced Serapis worship) the primitive Hellenic and Etruscan deities. In fact, long before this final triumph over the sceptical, Pliny appears disposed to accept Mithraicism, in its essential principle, as the only religion capable of satisfying a rational inquirer; as may be deduced from this noble passage (ii. 4) : "Eorum medius Sol fervidus, amplissima magnitudine, nec temporum modo terrarumque sed siderum etiam ipsorum cœlique Rector. Hanc esse mundi totius animam ac planius mentem, nunc principale Naturæ regimen ac *Numen* credere decet, opera ejus æstimantes. Hic lumen rebus ministrat, aufertque tenebras, hic reliqua

---

sidera occultat, illustrat; hic vices temporum annumque
semper renascentem ex usu Naturæ temperat, hic cœli tristi-
tiam discutit, atque etiam humani nubila animi serenat: hic
suum lumen cæteris quoque sideribus fœnerat; præclarus,
eximius, omnia intuens, omnia etiam exaudiens; at principi
literarum Homero placuisse in uno eo video. Quapropter
effigiem Dei formamque quærere imbecillitatis humanæ rear.
Quisquis est Deus, *si modo est alius*, et quacunque in parte, totus
est sensus, totus visus, totus auditus, totus animæ, totus animi,
totus sui." Thus, during the second and third centuries of the
Roman Empire, Mithras and Serapis had come almost to engross
the popular worship, even to the remotest limits of the known
world. For Mithraicism was originally the religion taught by
Zoroaster, although somewhat changed and materialized so
as better to assimilate itself to the previously established Nature
Worship of the West. Under this grosser form it took its name
from *Mithras*, who in the Zendavesta is not the Supreme Being
(Ormuzd), but the Chief of the subordinate Powers, the Seven
Amshaspands. Mithra is the Zend name for the sun, the
proper *mansion* of this Spirit, but not the Spirit himself. Hence
the great oath of Artaxerxes Mnemon was, "By the light of
Mithras," a counterpart of the tremendous adjuration of our
William the Conqueror, "By the Splendour of God!" But the
materialistic Greeks at once identified the Persian Spirit with
their own substantial Phœbus and Hyperion. Thus Ovid has,

"Placat equo Persis radiis Hyperiona cinctum." (Fasti I. 335.)

In this view of his nature Mithras was identified with other
types of the Sun-god, such as the "Phanaces" of Asia Minor,
and the "Dionysos" of Greece; and thereby soon usurped the
place of the latter in the long established Mysteries, the ancient
Dionysia. The importance into which the Mithraica had grown
by the middle of the second century may be estimated from a fact
mentioned by Lampridius, that the emperor himself (Commodus)
condescended to be initiated into them. Nay more, with their
penances, and tests of the courage of the neophyte, they may be
said to have been maintained by unbroken tradition through
the secret societies of the Middle Ages, then by the Rosicrucians,

down to that faint reflex of the latter, the Freemasonry of our own times. But this curious point must be reserved for the last Section of this Treatise investigating the nature of the last named societies. My present object is to point out the gradations by which the Mithraic principle passed into the Egyptian and semi-Christian forms of Gnosticism.

The mystic name *Abraxas* (asserted to have been the coinage of the Alexandrian Basilides) is said to mean either in actual Coptic "Holy Name" (as Bellermann will have it); or, as seems equally probable, is merely the Hebrew *Ha-Brachah* "Blessing," Grecised, in the same sense. That the symbolic figure embodying the idea of the Abraxas god has a reference to the sun in all its components is yet more evident, as shall be shown hereafter; similarly, the Brahmins apply their Ineffable Name *Aum* to the "fierce and all-pervading Sun"; and Macrobius devotes much curious learning to prove that all the great gods of antiquity, whatever their names and figures, were no more than various attempts at personifying the One Deity, whose residence is the sun. It must here be remembered that Basilides was by no means a *Christian heretic*, as the later Fathers found it expedient to represent him, but rather as his contemporary Clemens, relates, a philosopher devoted to the study of divine things; and thus possibly imbued with such Buddhistic notions as the intercourse between Alexandria and the cities of Guzerat (then ruled over by the Jaina kings) may have naturalized both in Egypt and in Palestine. This metropolis, as the grand emporium for foreign doctrines as well as foreign wares, supplies the reason for the frequent union of Mithras with Abraxas in the same stone, proceeding from the Alexandrian talisman-factory. A curious exemplification is a green jasper (Marlborough), bearing on one side the normal Zoroastrian device, Mithras slaughtering the Bull; on the other, the well-known Gnostic Pantheus. A truly Indian syncretism, which converts all deities from separate beings into mere deified attributes of one and the same God, and (for the initiated few, that is) reduces that seemingly unlimited polytheism into the acknowledgment of the existence of the Supreme Creator.

That model of a perfect prince, Severus Alexander, must have imbibed a strong tinge of the Gnosis (as indeed might have been expected from his birthplace and style of education), for although upon every *seventh day* he went up to worship in the Capitol, and also regularly visited the temples of the other Roman gods, he nevertheless " was intending to build a temple unto Christ, and to rank Him in the number of the gods. Which thing Hadrian also is said to have thought of, and actually to have ordered temples *without images* to be built in all the chief cities of the Empire : which same temples, because they contain no gods, are now called temples raised to Hadrian himself, although in reality he is reported to have prepared them for the purpose above-named. But he was prevented from carrying out his design by those who consulted the oracles (*sacra*), and discovered that, if it should be carried out, everybody would turn Christian, and thereby the other temples would be all deserted " (Lampridius i. 43). Indeed, there is every reason to believe that, as in the East, the worship of Serapis was at first combined with Christianity, and gradually merged into it with an entire change of name, though not of substance, carrying along with it many of its proper ideas and rites, so in the West the Mithras-worship produced a similar effect upon the character of the religion that took its place. Seel, in his admirable treatise upon Mithraicism ('Mithra,' p. 287) is of opinion that "as long as the Roman dominion lasted in Germany, we find traces there of the Mosaic law : and in the same way as there were single Jewish families, so were there single Christians existing amongst the heathen. The latter, however, for the most part, ostensibly paid worship to the Roman gods in order to escape persecution, holding secretly in their hearts the religion of Christ. It is by no means improbable that, under the permitted symbols of Mithras, they worshipped the Son of God, and the mysteries of Christianity. In this point of view, the Mithraic monuments, so frequent in Germany, are evidences to the faith of the early Christian Romans." This same supremacy of the Mithras-worship in his own times makes the grand scheme of Heliogabalus prove less insane than it strikes the modern reader at the first impression. He was intending (according to report) to permit no other worship at Rome than that of his own god and namesake, the Emesene aerolite, apt emblem of the Sun ; "bringing together in his temple the Fire of Vesta, the Palladium, the Ancilia, and all the other most venerated relics ; and moreover the *religion* of the Jews and Samaritans, and the *devotion** of the Christians." (Lampridius 3). To such a heterogeneous union that numerous section of the Roman public who shared Macrobius' sentiments on the nature of all ancient gods, could have found no possible objection so far as the *principle* was concerned.

That such a relationship to Christianity was actually alleged by the partisans of Mithraicism (when in its decline) is proved by the remarkable declaration of Augustine himself (John I. Dis. 7). "I remember that the priests of the *fellow in the cap* (*illius pileati*) used at one time to say, 'Our Capped One is himself a Christian.'" In this asserted affinity probably lay the motive that induced Constantine to adopt for the commonest type of his coinage (the sole currency of the Western provinces), and retain long after his conversion, the figure of Sol himself, with the legend "To the Invincible Sun, my companion (or guardian)." A type capable of a double interpretation, meaning equally the ancient Phœbus and the new Sun of Righteousness, and thereby unobjectionable to Gentile and Christian alike of the equally divided population amongst whom it circulated. Nay more, this Emperor when avowedly Christian, selected for the grandest ornament of his new Capital, a colossal Apollo, mounted upon a lofty column, which retained its place until cast down by an earthquake in the reign of Alexius Comnenus.

Through a similar interchange, the old festival held on the 25th day of December in honour of the "Birth-day of the Invincible One," and celebrated by the Great Games of the Circus (as marked in the Kalendar "viii KAL.IAN. N. INVICTI. C. M. xxiv†) was afterwards transferred to the commemoration of the Birth of Christ, of which the real day was, as the Fathers

---

* This curious distinction between "religio" and "devotio," is meant to mark the difference between a national and established creed and one held by individuals, without any public sanction.

† Signifying that twenty-four consecutive races of chariots were exhibited on that occasion in the Circus Maximus.

confess, totally unknown: Chrysostom, for example, declares (Hom. xxxi.) that the Birthday of Christ had then *lately* been fixed at Rome upon that day, in order that whilst the heathen were busied with their own profane ceremonies, the Christians might perform their holy rites without molestation.

And Mithras was the more readily admitted as the type of Christ, Creator and Maintainer of the Universe, inasmuch as the Zendavesta declares him to be the First Emanation of Ormuzd, the Good Principle, and the Manifestation of Himself unto the world. Now it was from this very creed that the Jews, during their long captivity in the Persian Empire (of which when restored to Palestine they formed but a province), derived all the angelology of their religion, even to its minutest details, such as we find it flourishing in the times of the Second Kingdom. Not until then are they discovered to possess the belief in a future state; of rewards and punishments, the latter carried on in a fiery lake; the existence of a complete hierarchy of good and evil angels, taken almost verbatim from the lists given by the Zendavesta; the soul's immortality, and the Last Judgment—all of them essential parts of the Zoroastrian scheme, and recognised by Josephus as the fundamental doctrines of the Judaism of his own times.

To all these ideas Moses in the Law makes not the slightest allusion; his promises and threatenings are all of the earth, earthy; he preaches a religion of *Secularists,* and such a religion was, down to the latest days of Jerusalem, still maintained by the Sadducees. Now these Sadducees were the most ancient and respectable families of the nation, who boasted of keeping the law of Moses pure, and uncontaminated from the admixture of foreign notions imbibed by the commonalty during their long sojourn amongst the Gentiles. Nay more, there is some reason to accept Matter's etymology of the name of their opponents, the Pharisees, as actually signifying " Persians," being a term of contempt for the holders of the new-fangled doctrines picked up from their conquerors. And this etymology is a much more rational one, and more consistent with the actual elements of the word, than the common one making it to mean " Separatists " —an epithet by no means applicable to a party constituting the immense *majority* of the race. It is only necessary now to allude to the ingenious theory of Bishop Warburton, set forth in his 'Divine Legation of Moses,' who converts the absence of all spiritualism from his teaching into the strongest argument for its being directly inspired from Heaven.

But from whatever source derived, how closely does the Zoroastrian idea of the nature and office of Mithras coincide with the definition of those of Christ as given by the author of the Epistle to the Hebrews, that profound Jewish theologian, who styles Him the "Brightness (or *reflection*) of his glory, the express *image** of his person, upholding all things by the word of his power;" and again, "being made so much better than the angels as he hath by inheritance obtained a more excellent *Name* than they," and here it may be observed that the *Reflection* of the *Invisible* Supreme in his First Emanation is a distinguishing feature in most of the Gnostic systems. Mithras used to be invoked *together* with the Sun, and thus, being confounded with that luminary, became the object of a separate worship, which ultimately superseded that of Ormuzd himself: and this was the only one propagated by the Pontic colonists and their converts amongst the nations of the West. Secondary deities often usurp the places of those of the first rank; so Vishnu and Siva have entirely eclipsed Brahma. Serapis had played the same part with the Pharaonic gods of Egypt, and yet more striking analogies from modern creeds are too obvious to require quotation. Through this relationship of ideas Mithraic symbolism found its way into early Christian art in many of its particulars. The bas-relief over the portal of the Baptistery at Parma (a work of the 12th century), has all the aspect of a Mithraic monument, and certainly its design would be very difficult to understand from a Scriptural point of view.

---

* 'Απαύγασμα—χαρακτήρ, the latter word literally "impression of a seal," is the exact counterpart of the Hebrew title, "Tikkan," the Primal Emanation.

II. THE MITHRAIC SACRAMENTS.

The principal rites of the worship of Mithras bore a very curious resemblance to those subsequently established in the Catholic church; they likewise furnished a model for the initiatory ceremonies observed by the secret societies of the Middle Ages, and by their professed descendants in modern times. The Neophytes were admitted by the rite of *Baptism;* the initiated at their assemblies solemnly celebrated a species of *Eucharist:* whilst the courage and endurance of the candidate for admission into the sect were tested by *twelve* consecutive trials, called "The Tortures," undergone within a cave constructed for the purpose; all which "tortures" had to be completely passed through before participation in the Mysteries was granted to the aspirant.

The two distinguishing Rites, or "Sacraments" (to use the technical term) are thus alluded to by Justin Martyr (*Apol.* II) in the earliest description which has been left us of their character. "The Apostles in the Commentaries written by themselves, which we call *Gospels*, have delivered down to us that Jesus thus commanded them: He having taken bread, after that He had given *thanks*,[*] said : Do this in commemoration of me ; this is my body. Also having taken a cup and returned thanks, He said : This is my blood, and delivered it unto them alone. Which things indeed the evil spirits have taught to be done, out of memory, in the Mysteries and Initiations of Mithras. For in these likewise a cup of water, and bread, are set out, with the addition of certain words, in the sacrifice or act of worship of the person about to be initiated : a thing which Ye either know by personal experience or may learn by inquiry." Again, Tertullian, writing in the following century, has in the same connection : "The Devil, whose business it is to pervert the truth, *mimicks the exact circumstances* of the Divine Sacraments, in the Mysteries of idols. He himself *baptises* some that is to say, his believers and followers ; he promises forgive-

---

[*] This expression seems to prove that the notion of *blessing*, or consecrating, the elements, had not then (the second century) crept into the Christian practice.

ness of sins from the *Sacred Fount*, and thereby initiates them into the religion of Mithras : thus he *marks on the forehead* his own soldiers : there he celebrates the *oblation of bread :* he brings in the symbol of the Resurrection, and wins the crown with the sword." By the " symbol of the Resurrection" Tertullian clearly means that " simulation of death" mentioned by Lampridius (of which more hereafter), and which is typified on so many talismans by the corpse bestridden by the Solar Lion. The final ceremony he has himself explained in another passage : " Blush, my Roman fellow-soldiers, even though ye be not to be judged by Christ, but by any ' Soldier of Mithras,' who when he is undergoing initiation in the *Cave*, in the very Camp of the Powers of Darkness, when the *crown* (garland, rather) is offered to him (a sword being placed between, as though in semblance of martyrdom), and about to be set upon his head, is instructed to put forth his hand, and push the crown away, transferring it perchance, to his shoulder, saying at the same time : My crown is Mithras. And from that time forth he never wears a crown (garland), and this he has for the badge of his initiation, for he is immediately known to be a ' soldier of Mithras,' if he rejects a garland when offered to him, saying that his crown is his god. Let us therefore acknowledge the craftiness of the Devil ; who copies certain things of those that be Divine, in order that he may confound and judge us by the faithfulness of his own followers." As to the ceremony here mentioned, unimportant as it may seem to the modern reader, it may be remarked that as the wearing a garland was indispensable among the ancients on all festive occasions, the refusal of one upon such occasions would be a most conspicuous mark of singularity, and of unflinching profession of faith. But every dispassionate observer will perceive that these over-zealous Fathers proceed to beg the question when they assume that the Mithraic rites were devised as *counterfeits* of the Christian Sacraments: inasmuch as the former were in existence long before the first promulgation of Christianity ; unless indeed to *imitate* by anticipation be considered as merely another proof of the mischievous sagacity of its diabolical opponent. On the other hand, there is good reason to suspect that the simple commemorative, or distinctive, ceremonies, instituted by the first founder of Christianity, were gradually invested with those mystic and supernatural virtues which later ages insisted upon as articles of faith, by the teaching of unscrupulous missionaries, anxious to outbid the attractions of long-established rites of an apparently cognate character. By this assimilation they offered to their converts through the performance of, as it were, certain magical practices, all those spiritual blessings of which the rites themselves were, at their institution, the *symbols* only, not the instruments. A very instructive illustration of such union of Mithraicism and Christianity, in the celebration of the Eucharist, is afforded by the Pistis-Sophia's description of the great one celebrated by the Saviour himself upon the shore of the Sea of Galilee, which will be found given at length in its proper place. And lastly, it deserves to be mentioned that " eating the flesh and drinking the blood " of a human sacrifice was far from being a mere figure of speech in certain of these mystic celebrations. Pliny gives high praise to Claudius for having suppressed the worship of the Druids (whom he considers as identical in their religion with the Magi), in whose rites "it was esteemed the highest act of religion to slaughter a man, and the most salutary of proceedings to eat the flesh of the same." And in this notion, which necessarily became attached by suspicion to the proceedings of all secret societies, lay most probably the root of the belief so widely diffused amongst the Roman vulgar, that the real Eucharist of the first Christians at their nocturnal meetings was the sacrifice, and the feasting upon, a new-born child, concealed within a vessel of flour, into which the catechumen was directed by his sponsors to plunge a knife.

In the particulars preserved to us of the Mithraic Sacrament, certain very curious analogies to those of the Christian rite cannot fail to arrest our attention. The " Bread therein used was a round cake," emblem of the solar disk, and called *Mizd*. In this name Seel discovers the origin of *Missa*, as designating the Bloodless Sacrifice of the Mass, assuming that this Mizd was the prototype of the Host (*hostia*), which is of precisely the same form and dimensions.

It is not out of place to notice here the various etymologies which have been proposed for the word *Missa.* The most popular one, which moreover has the sanction of Ducange, derives it from the words "Ite, missa est," with which the priest dismissed the *non-communicant* part of the congregation, before proceeding to the actual consecration of the Eucharist. The translation of the phrase by the vulgar into "Depart, it is the Missa," would certainly be obvious enough. But, according to the rule in all such cases, the *object* sacrificed gives its name to the ceremony, rather than a phrase from the ceremonial itself, and this object had from time immemorial gone by the name of *hostia,* or "victim." The early Christians were quite as partial as the Gnostics to the naturalizing of the Hebrew terms belonging to the Mosaic ordinances, and applying the same to their own practices. Thus the old Covenant went amongst them by the name of *Phase,* for example :—

> "In hoc festo novi Regis,
> Novum *Pascha* novæ legis
> Vetus *Phase* terminat."

The Rabbins have possibly preserved a tradition that explains the true origin of the wafer. Alphonsus de Spira, in his "Fortalitium Fidei" (II. 2), asserts that its circular form is a symbol of the sun, and that it is in reality offered in sacrifice, at the celebration of the Mass, to the genius of that luminary! For the Kabbalists hold that Moses and the prophets were inspired by the genius of Saturn, a good and pure spirit, whereas Jesus was by that of Mercury, a malevolent one ; and the Christian religion was the work of Mercury, Jupiter and the Sun, all combining together for that purpose. There is yet another curious analogy to be noticed, when it is remembered that the Mass symbolises the *death* of its first institutor. A *round* cake (the *chupatty* of such evil notoriety at the commencement of the Sepoy Mutiny) is, amongst the Hindoos, the established offering to the Manes of their ancestors. The Christian "breaking of bread," besides symbolising the great sacrifice once offered, seems, from the account of the Manifestation at Emmaus, to have been done in some peculiar way which should serve for a *masonic* token, or means of mutual recognition amongst the brethren.

The sacramental Cup, or *chalice*, is often represented as set upon the Mithraic altar, or rather, *table;* and a curious piece of jugglery connected with its employment (though not amongst the Mithraicists), is described by Epiphanius (Hæres. xxxiv.). The followers of Marcus, in their celebrating the Eucharist, employed *three* vases made of the clearest glass. These were filled with wine which, during the progress of the ceremony, changed into a blood-red, purple, and blue colour, respectively. " Thereupon the officiating minister, or more properly speaking, *magician,* hands one of these vessels to some lady of the congregation, and requests her to bless it. Which done, he pours this into another vase of much greater capacity, with the prayer, " May the grace of God, which is above all, inconceivable, inexplicable, fill thine inner man, and increase the knowledge of Himself within thee, sowing the grain of mustard-seed in good ground !" Whereupon the liquid in the larger vase swells and swells until it runs over the brim.

The worship of Mithras long kept its ground under the Christian emperors in the capital itself, and doubtless survived its overthrow there for many generations longer in the remote and then semi-independent provinces. At the very close of the fourth century, Jerome, writing to Læta, says, " A *few* years ago, did not your kinsman Gracchus, a name the very echo of patrician nobility, when holding the office of Prefect of the City, break down and burn the Cave of Mithras, with all the monstrous images which pervade the initiatory rites, as Corax, Niphus, the Soldier, the Lion, the Persian, Helios, and Father Bromius ? "

In the imagery here alluded to, it is easy to recognise figures that perpetually occur upon the still extant representations of the Mithras worship. In *Corax*, the Raven; in *Niphus*, Cneph the serpent; the *armed man;* the *Lion* bestriding the human victim; the youth in *Persian* garb; the *Sun,* expressed either by Phœbus in his car, or by the star with eight rays; and *Bromius* " the Roarer," appropriate title of the Grecian Dionysos; who also appears as the Asiatic *Phanaces,* a youth holding a torch in each hand, one elevated and one depressed to signify his rising and setting. Chiflet's gem (Fig. 62) may on good grounds be taken for a picture of the Mithraic ritual, and upon it all the forementioned figures and symbols are easily to be discovered. Two erect serpents form a kind of frame to the whole tableau ; at the top of which are seen the heads of Sol and Luna confronted ; between them stands an eagle with outspread wings ; at the back of each, a raven. In the field are two naked, crowned men on horseback, trampling upon as many dead bodies; between them a kneeling figure in supplicatory attitude, over whose head are two stars. Behind each horseman stand two soldiers. In the exergue is set out a table supporting a loaf, a fawn (sacred to Bacchus), a chalice, and something indistinct, but probably meant for the *crown* Tertullian speaks of. The reverse presents a more simple design : two crested serpents (*dracones*), twined about wands, and looking into a cup; two stars over a table resting upon a larger vase; and on each side a bow, the ends of which finish in serpents' heads.

In this composition we probably see portrayed certain amongst the tests of the neophyte's courage, which, according to Suidas, were termed the "Twelve Degrees" or "Tortures." These corresponded in nature, although of vastly more severe reality, with those trials of courage to which our Masonic Lodges subject the "apprentice" who seeks admission amongst them. During the Mithraic probation, which lasted *forty* days,[*] the candidate was tested by the Four Elements, he lay naked a certain number of nights upon the snow, and afterwards was scourged for the space of two days. These Twelve Tortures are sculptured upon the border of the famous Mithraic tablets preserved in the Innsbruck Museum, and a brief account of their several stages will serve to elucidate much of what remains to be discussed. I. Man standing and about to plunge a dagger into the throat of a kneeling figure, who holds up his hands in supplication. (This scene appears analogous to the one in the modern ceremonial, when the candidate, ordered to remove the bandage from his eyes, beholds many swords pointed in the

_____
[*] Perhaps the origin of the Lenten term of self-inflicted punishment.

most threatening manner at his naked breast.) II. Naked man lying on the earth, his head resting on his hand, in the posture of repose. (Probably the penance of the bed of snow.) III. The same figure, standing with hands uplifted in a huge crescent (perhaps an *ark*, and representing the trial by water. To this last, Plato is reported to have been subjected during his initiation in Egypt, and to have but narrowly escaped drowning). IV. The same, but now with the *pileus*, cap of liberty, upon his head, rushing boldly into a great fire (the trial by fire). V. He is now seen struggling through a deep stream, and endeavouring to grasp a rock. VI. Bull walking to the left.

On the other side come the remaining stages. VII. Four guests reclining at a horseshoe table (*sigma*), upon which is set a boar roasted whole. VIII. Youth guided up a flight of interminable steps by an aged man. IX. Youth kneeling before a man in a long robe, whose hand he grasps in prayer. X. The same figures, but their positions are interchanged. XI. Seated man, before whom kneels a naked, crowned, youth, escorted by one in a long robe. XII. Naked man holding up the hind legs of a cow, so as to receive in his face the stream still regarded by the Hindoos as the most efficient laver of regeneration, and consequently always administered to persons at their last gasp. The same sacred fluid (as I am informed by a Parsee) is used in the sacramental cups drunk by every male upon his first admission into that religion, which takes place on his completing his seventh year. Nay more, such is the belief in its cleansing virtue, that scrupulous Parsees always carry a bottle thereof in their pocket, wherewith to purify their hands after any unavoidable contact with unbelievers!

Very similar ceremonies to these were practised in the secret societies of the Middle Ages, if we choose to accept Von Hammer's interpretation of certain mysterious sculptures, still to be seen in the Templar-churches of Germany; and which he has copiously illustrated in his 'Mysterium Baphometis revelatum.' In the intaglio already described, the kneeling neophyte is encompassed by all the terrific and mysterious host of Mithras, so remorselessly destroyed by the zealous Gracchus.

And again, the corpses trampled on by the crowned horsemen clearly refer to that recorded test of the candidate's fortitude—the apparent 'approach of death—for Lampridius puts down amongst the other mad freaks of Commodus, that during the Mithraic ceremonies, "when a certain thing had to be done for the purpose of inspiring terror, he polluted the rites by a *real murder :* " an expression clearly showing that a scenic representation of such an act did really form a part of the proceedings. The *Raven* properly takes its place here, as being the attribute of the Solar god in the Hellenic creed, on which account it is often depicted standing upon Apollo's lyre.

Many other gems express the spiritual benefits conferred by the Mithraic initiation upon believers. A frequent device of the kind, is a man, with hands bound behind his back, seated at the foot of a pillar supporting a gryphon with paw on wheel, that special emblem of the solar god; often accompanied with the legend ΔΙΚΑΙΩΣ, " I have deserved it." Another (Blacas) displays an unusual richness of symbolism : the same gryphon's tail ends in a scorpion, whilst the wheel squeezes out of its chrysalis a tiny human soul that stretches forth its hands in jubilation ; in front stands Thoth's ibis, holding in its beak the balance, perhaps the horoscope of the patient. This talisman too, unites the Egyptian with the Magian creed, for the benefit of the carrier; for the reverse displays Isis, but in the character of Hygieia, standing upon her crocodile ; the field being occupied by strangely complicated monograms, of sense intelligible to the initiated alone, and doubtless communicated to the recipient of the talisman, who found in them "a New Name written, that no man knoweth, save he that receiveth the same." But both doctrines and ceremonial of this religion are best understood through the examination of extant representations displaying them either directly or allegorically ; which in their turn are illustrated by the practice of the faithful few who still keep alive the Sacred Fire, namely the Parsees of Guzerat. The series therefore will be most fittingly opened by the following curious description of a cave of Mithras, as discovered in its original and unprofaned condition, written by that eminent antiquary, Flaminius Vacca. (No. 117.)

K

III.   A ROMAN MITHRAS IN HIS CAVE.

" I remember there was found in the vineyard of Sig. Orazio Muti (where the treasure was discovered), opposite S. Vitale, an idol in marble about 5 palms high (3¾ ft.), standing erect upon a pedestal in an empty chamber, which had the door walled up. This idol had the head of a lion, but the body that of a man. Under the feet was a globe, whence sprung a serpent which encompassed all the idol, and its head entered into the lion's mouth. He had his hands crossed upon the breast, with a key in each; four wings fastened upon the shoulders, two pointing upwards, two downwards. I do not consider it a very antique work, being done in a rude manner, or else indeed it was so ancient that at the time when it was made the good style was not yet known. Sig. Orazio, however, told me that a theologian, a Jesuit Father, explained its meaning by saying it signified the Devil, who, in the times of heathenism, ruled over the world : hence the *globe* under his feet, the *serpent* which begirt his body and entered into his mouth, signified his foretelling the future with ambiguous responses; the *keys* in his hands, his sovereignty over the world ; the *lion's head*, his being the ruler of all beasts ; the *wings*, his presence everywhere. Such was the interpretation given by the Father aforesaid. I have done everything to see the idol, but Sig. Orazio being now dead, his heirs do not know what has become of it. It is not, however, unlikely that by the advice of the same theologian, Sig. Orazio may have sent it to some *limekiln to cure its dampness*, for it had been buried many and many a year." Thus was this most interesting monument destroyed through the conceited ignorance of a wretched ecclesiastic, himself more truly a worshipper of the Evil Principle, than was the ancient votary of the beneficent Lord of Light who carved that wondrous image. Vacca adds, " I remember, there was found in the same place, after the above-mentioned idol, another, only in bas-relief, also having a lion's head, but the rest of the body human : with the arms extended, in each hand a torch; with two wings pointing upwards, two downwards, from between which issued a serpent.

At his right stood an altar with fire;. from the idol's mouth proceeded a ribbon or scroll extending over the fire."

This *lion*-headed deity can be no other than Jerome's "Pater Bromius," a Grecian title of Bacchus; and he, we are told, distinguished himself under that disguise in the famous war of the giants—

> " Tu cum Parentis regna per arduum
> Cohors Gigantum scanderet impia,
> Rhætum retorsisti *leonis*
>   Unguibus horribilique mala."
>
> (Horace, Od. II. xix. 21–24.)

And, tracing back this composite figure to the real source of such iconology, it is found to be the very one under which " Nri-singha-avatar " is depicted.   It was assumed by the deity in order to destroy the tyrant Hiransyakaçipu, who had obtained the gift of invulnerability against all *known* beasts, either by day or night.

A Mithraic cave, with the contiguous buildings, was discovered at Spoleto in 1878.   In the end wall were the usual three niches for the god and his torch-bearers.   In front of them an altar inscribed " Soli invicto Mithræ sacrum."   Close to the altar, a tall phallic stone, perforated with a square hole near the top—perhaps the " stone symbolizing the Birth of Mithras " mentioned by Firmicus.   The cave, with the ground plan of the whole edifice is given in the ' Archæologia,' vol. 47, p. 205.

IV. MITHRAIC TALISMANS.

Mithraic gems are, for the most part, earlier in date than those emanating from the Gnosticism of Alexandria, with whose doctrines they had no connection whatever in their first origin. Little difficulty will be found on inspection in separating the two classes, the former being pointed out by the superiority of their style, and yet more so by the absence of the Egyptian symbols, and long Coptic legends that generally accompany the latter.   Indeed many of them belong to the best period of Roman art—the age of Hadrian ; and it is easy to perceive how the worship of Apollo gradually merged into that of his more spiritual oriental representative, in the times when religious ideas of Indian origin began to get the upper hand throughout the Roman world—a religion essentially speculative, and dealing with matters pertaining to another life and the Invisible, utterly different in nature from the old Grecian creed, so materialistic, so active, so entirely busying itself with the Present and the Visible.

In accordance with the rule that prescribed the proper *material* for talismans, the Jasper (Pliny's *Molochites*), green, mottled, or yellow, is almost exclusively employed for intagli embodying Mithraic ideas, and which take the place of Phœbus and his attributes amongst the glyptic remains of the second and third centuries. To judge from their fine execution, certain examples of the class may even date from the age of the first Cæsars, and thus form as it were the advanced guard of that countless host of regular Gnostic works, amidst whose terrific barbarism ancient art ultimately expires. In their beginning these Mithraic works were the fruit of the modified Zoroastrian doctrines so widely disseminated over the Empire after the conquest of Pontus—doctrines whose grand feature was the exclusive worship of the Solar god, as the fountain of all life—a notion philosophically true, if indeed the vital principle be, as some scientists assert, nothing more than electricity. As will be shown hereafter (" Serapis "), the later Platonists, like Macrobius, laboured hard to demonstrate that the multitudinous divinities of the old faiths, wheresoever established, were no other than various epithets and expressions for the same god in his different phases. The aim of all the school was to accommodate the old faith to the influence of the Buddhistic theosophy, the very essence of which was that the innumerable gods of the Hindoo mythology were but *names* for the *Energies* of the First Triad in its successive *Avatars*, or manifestations unto man.

To come now to the actual types setting forth these ideas ; prominent amongst them is the figure of the *Lion* (he being in astrological parlance the " House of the Sun "), usually surrounded with stars, and carrying in his jaws a bull's head, emblem of earth subjected to his power. Sometimes he tramples on the serpent, which in this connection no longer typifies wisdom, but the Principle of Evil. For in all religions emanating from the East, where deadly poisonousness is the most conspicuous character of the snake-tribe, the reptile has been adopted as the most speaking type of the *Destroyer*. In the West, on the other hand, where the same species is for the most part innocuous, and a mere object of wonder, it has always symbolized wisdom, and likewise eternity, from the popular belief in the yearly removal of its youth through casting the slough; on this account the serpent was made the companion of Apollo and Aesculapius; and furthermore plays so important a part in Scandinavian mythology, holding the whole universe together in its perpetual embrace.

Mithras himself often makes his appearance, figured as a youthful Persian, plunging the national weapon, " Medus acinaces," into the throat of a prostrate bull (which expresses the same doctrine as the type last mentioned), whilst overhead are the sun and moon, the group standing in the centre of the Zodiac. But the completest assembly of Mithraic figures and symbols that has come under my notice, is the intaglio published by Caylus ('Recueil d'Antiquités,' vi. pl. 84). It is engraved upon a very fine agate, $2 \times 1\frac{1}{2}$ inches in measurement. In the centre is the usual type of Mithras slaughtering the Bull, the tail of which terminates in three wheat-ears, and between the hind legs hangs a huge scorpion; below is the Lion strangling the Serpent—emblem of darkness and of death. On each side stands a fir-tree, admitted into this system because its spiry form imitates a flame, for which same reason its cone was taken for the symbol of the element fire, and therefore borne in the hands of deities in the most ancient Syrian sculptures. Against these fir-trees are affixed torches, one pointing upwards, the other downwards, which clearly stand for the rising and setting of the Sun. At the side of one is a scorpion, of the other, a bull's head. Above each tree again is a torch, each pointing in an opposite direction. The principal group is flanked by Phœbus in his four-horse, Luna in her two-horse car. Above the whole stand two winged figures entwined with serpents and leaning upon long sceptres, between whom rise up three flames, besides four more at the side of the right-hand figure, making up the mystic number seven—perhaps repre senting the seven Amshaspands or Archangels. A naked female, surrounded with stars, kneels before the angel on the left—doubtless the soul for whose benefit the talisman was composed—soliciting his patronage.

Could this elaborate composition be interpreted, it would certainly be found to contain a summary of the Mithraic creed as it was received by the nations of the West. As it is, however, some portions of the tableau are explained by certain legends to be found in the Parsee sacred books ; whilst others derive light from comparison with the larger monuments of the same worship. Thus, the termination of the bull's tail in ears of wheat allude to the fifty life-giving plants which sprang from the tail of the Primæval *Bull* (or *Life*, the same word in Zend) after he had been slain by Ahriman. Of the same animal the seed was carried up by the Izeds (genii) to the Moon, where, purified in her beams, it was moulded by Ormuzd into a new pair, the parents of all that exists in earth, air and water. The scorpion is appended to the part of the body, properly under the influence of the sign so called, for as Manilius teaches, "The fiery scorpion in the *groin* delights." In this particular situation it expresses Autumn, as the serpent underneath does Winter ; and with good reason takes the place of the bull's genitals, for, as the same poet sings (iv. 217.)

> "With fiery tail when Scorpio threatens war,
> As through the stars he drives the solar car,
> He searches earth with penetrating rays
> And the mixed seed deep in her furrows lays."

The torches raised and lowered signify the East and West. In the circular altar of the Villa Borghese (Winckelmann Mon. Ined. No. 21) the bust of Luna appears resting on a crescent over an aged head in front face with crabs' claws springing out of his forehead—a speaking type of Oceanus. The bust of the *rising* sun, with his customary badge, the eight-rayed star, in point, rests upon an erect flambeau, whilst that of the *setting* luminary looking downwards, is placed upon another lowered towards earth. Again, the serpent winding *four* times about the figures may signify the sun's annual revolution ; an explanation rendered the more plausible by the torso of Mithras at Arles, in which the Zodiacal Signs occupy the intervals between the coils of the same serpent. The lion and raven stand for the attendant priests; for in these mysteries the higher officials were denominated *Lions*, the lower *Ravens*: whence the rites themselves got the name of " Leontica," and " Coracica."

The fires, the planets and the genii presiding over them are in number *seven*—a numeral the most sacred of all amongst the Persians. But of these seven Fires, *three* are ever depicted in a special manner as those most worthy to be held in reverence. These three are the " Fire of the Stars," that is, of the planet Venus, named *Anahid;* the " Fire of the Sun," or the Fire *Mihr;* and the " Fire of Lightning," or the Fire *Bersiov*, that is, the planet Jupiter. The *Mihr* is the winged orb, so common in all Assyrian sculpture—an emblem which serves to explain the Prophet's simile, " the *Sun* of Righteousness with healing in his *wings*."

The worship of the Fire Gushtasp (or that of Anahid) figures on the Zend sculptures as a very ancient worship, and also in the " Shah Nameh ; " just as that of the goddess Anaitis does in many Greek authors from Herodotus downwards. This historian observes (I. 131) that *at first* the Persians worshipped only the sun, moon, and elements, until they learnt from the Assyrians the worship of Venus Urania, whom they called *Mitra*, the same being the Mylitta of the Babylonians, the Alata or Alilat of the Arabians. Now Mitra (feminine of Mithras) and Anahid, are one and the same goddess, that is to say, the Morning Star, a female Genius, presiding over love, giving light, and directing the harmonious movement of the other planets by the sound of her lyre, the strings whereof are the solar rays—" Apollo's lyre strung with his golden hair " (Creuzer, Kal. de l'Antiq. ii. 731). In this doctrine we discover the reason for the *separation* of the Fires upon Caylus' gem into *two* groups; the principal group consisting of the three most anciently adored ; the subsidiary one of the remaining four.

Other Mithraic symbols are of a very speaking character, and almost explain their own meaning at first sight. Thus Mithras *piercing* the bull's throat with his dagger signifies the *penetration* of the solar ray into the bosom of the earth, by whose action all Nature is nourished ; as is further expressed by the *Dog's* licking up the blood that pours from the wound. The sign Capricorn frequently introduced into the same group, declares the necessity of *moisture* to co-operate with the Sun's influence in bringing about the germination of the seed sown ; whilst the *scorpion*, in the significant position above noticed, expresses the generative *heat*. The union of two diverse religions, already mentioned, is curiously exemplified by those stones that show the Mithraic group surrounded by sets of the sacred animals of *Egypt*, arranged by threes—crocodiles, goats, calves, vultures, hawks, ibises—standing around in attitudes of adoration, and gazing upon the great work of their supreme lord, Mithras (see page 41, fig. 2).

Mithraic bas-beliefs cut upon the smoothed faces of rocks, or upon tablets of stone, still abound throughout the former western provinces of the Roman Empire ; many exist in Germany ; still more in France; others in this island, along the line of the Picts' Wall, and a remarkably fine example at York, the station of the Sixth Legion. The famous " Arthur's Oon " (destroyed in the last century) upon the Carron, a hemispherical vaulted building of immense blocks of stone, was unmistakably a *Specus Mithraicum*—the same in design as Chosroes' magnificent Fire temple at Gazaca. Inasmuch as the sun-god was the chief deity * of the Druids, it is easy to imagine what ready acceptance the worship of his more refined Persian equivalent would find amongst the Celtic Aborigines, when once introduced by the Roman troops and colonists, many of whom were Orientals. To the last circumstance a curious testimony is incidentally borne by Lampridius, when he remarks that the entire military force employed by Maximinus in his great in-

---

* As " Belenus " he continued to the last the patron-god of Aquileia, that Gallic metropolis of Cisalpine Gaul, and to his power was ascribed the death of Maximin when besieging that city. The acclamations of the senate on the receipt of the news of their deliverance from the tyrant, prove that Belenus was held to be another name for Apollo. A *shoe* of the giant emperor, a convincing testimony, literally an " ex pede Herculem," to his incredible stature, was yet to be seen in the days of Lampridius, nailed to a tree in the *sacred grove* at the place of his fall.

vasion of Germany, was the same that had been raised by Severus Alexander, and which had accompanied him to the scene of his murder, "either the North of Gaul or *Britain*," which same army the historian describes as "potentissimus quidem per *Armenios* et *Osrhoenos*, et *Parthos*, et omnis generis hominum." For this sagacious emperor had appointed to subordinate commands in his own army all the prisoners of royal or noble birth whom he had taken in his preceding Persian campaign.

Although the modern Parsees, like their Achæmenian ancestry in the days of Herodotus, abominate idols and all visible representations of things divine, yet do they still piously cherish the ideas embodied on the sculptures just passed under review. Amongst these, most conspicuous is their veneration for the *Dog* which they yet esteem the most holy of animals. Tavernier (I. 493) was on this account greatly scandalised by the Guebres of Surat; "they have another strange custom—when a person is on the point of death, to take a little dog, and place it upon his breast. When they perceive that he is at his last gasp, they apply the dog's muzzle to the dying man's mouth, and make it bark twice when in this position, as if they meant to make the person's soul enter into the dog,* which they pretend will deliver it unto the angel appointed to receive the same. Moreover, if a dog happens to die, they carry it out of the town, and pray to God in behalf of that piece of carrion, as though the brute's soul could derive any advantage from their prayers after its death." Following up this analogy, the sculptured dog licking up the bull's blood may actually be intended for such a vehicle of departing life. In these times the Parsees expose their dead, upon gratings laid on the summit of the "Tower of silence," to be consumed by the birds alone; but under the Sassanian monarchy it was the inviolable rule to lay out all corpses in the open fields to be devoured by the dogs. This was no more than carrying out to the full a very ancient principle of the Zoroastrian religion. Herodotus (I. 140) states from his own knowledge that the corpse of a Magus was not allowed to be buried before it had been *attacked* by a bird or

* My Parsee informant assures me this ceremony is now modified into the merely bringing a dog into the dying man's chamber.

dog; adding that the same was *reported* of the other Persians.
The Magi regarded the killing of a dog equally criminal with
that of a human being   This primitive style of obsequies the
Sassanians strove hard to enforce upon all nations subjected to
their sway, viewing as a great sacrilege the placing of dead
bodies in the bosom of the earth; a still greater, the consuming
them by the sacred element, *Fire.* This practice above all
others scandalised the narrow-minded Byzantines; the historian
Agathias expressing his horror at the casting the dead to the
dogs, whatever their rank or dignity in life; as in the case of
the great Satrap Mermeroes, whom he *saw* thus exposed naked
in the fields to be so devoured.   When the last seven sages of
Greece, expelled from their professional chairs at Athens by the
stupid bigotry of Justinian, sought refuge in the ostentatious
hospitality of Nushirwan the Just, even they (despite their
philosophy) found themselves obliged, by their disgust at the
sight of this practice,* to return home with sad loss of dignity,
and submit to the spirit of the times.   If the dogs refused to
touch the carcase, this was looked on by the friends of the
deceased as the very worst of indications as to the ultimate
destination of his soul.   The Parsees, who, with more decency,
constitute the raven† (or equally sacred creature) sexton and
sepulchre in one, derive a similar augury from observing
which eye is first attacked by the bird, the preference for the
right one being the token of salvation; for the left, of the
reverse.

A very curious portion of the initiatory ceremony in the

* To which they would have been
forced to conform had they continued
under the protection of the Sassanian
king.

† The same practice prevails in
Thibet with the motive thus assigned.
"Several bodies exposed on the
banks of the stream were being devoured by crows and buzzards, which
soon leave nothing but the skeletons,
which are washed away by the sum-
mer rise of the stream.   The Tibe-
tians believe that as each buzzard,
gorged with its foul repast, soars
into the heavens, a portion of the
spirit of the deceased is taken up
into heaven.   In the case of rich
people Lamas are employed to divide
the body into small pieces and carry
it up to the top of a hill, where the
vulture and buzzard soon dispose of
it.   Interment of the dead is also
practised, but only among the poorer
people, who cannot afford to pay
Lamas to perform the ceremony of
exposing the body."—Cooper's 'Tra-
vels of a Pioneer of Commerce,'
p. 270.

ancient Mysteries was the giving of the "Mark of Mithras."
After successfully undergoing each stage of the ordeal, the
accepted candidate was *marked* in a certain indelible manner,
but the exact nature of this marking cannot now be ascertained
The expressions used by St. Augustine (in Johan. i. dis. 7) lead
us to conclude two things : firstly, that the *engraved stones*, the
object of our consideration, were given to the candidate at the
end of his probation, for a token of admission into the fra-
ternity, and for a medium of recognition between members :
and secondly, that every one, upon admission, was stamped with
a *secret Mark*, indelibly imprinted in his flesh. "Something of
the sort has been copied by a certain Spirit, in that he will
have his *own image* to be purchased with *blood*, forasmuch as he
was aware that mankind were some day or another to be
redeemed by the shedding of blood." This last expression
shows that this Mark was not *burnt in*, but *incised* or tattooed ;
and the same conclusion may be deduced from St. John's using
the term χάραγμα, *engraving*, not στίγμη, *branding*, for that badge
of servitude which all the subjects of the Second Beast, " having
horns like a lamb's, and speaking like a dragon," were forced to
receive, either *in* their right hands (i.e., upon the palm) or upon
their foreheads, and he caused all, both small and great, rich
and poor, free and bond, to receive a Mark in their right hand,
or in their foreheads : " and that no man might buy or sell, save
he that had the Mark, or the Name of the Beast, or the Number
of his Name " (Rev. xiii. 17). These words contain a com-
pendious account of the different kinds of " Stigmata " then in
use to distinguish those devoting themselves to any particular
deity. The *Mark* was the figure of the special symbol or
attribute of that deity (exactly answering to the caste-marks of
the modern Hindoos) : the *Name* was his own, written at full
length in some sacred language : the *Number* was the more
recondite way of expressing that name, either by a single
numeral in the primitive Chaldæan fashion, or by other letters
taken numerically, and yielding the same sum. The author of
the Apocalypse very probably had the Mithraicists in view
when penning this allegory ; yet we may be certain that the
members of a *secret* society did not receive the mark of member-

ship upon any *conspicuous* part of their persons. The same necessity meets us here, as in every other branch of this inquiry, for placing the origin of all such sectarian bodily Marks in India—the true fountainhead, directly or indirectly, of so many Gnostic practices. *There*, the votaries of the several deities are still distinguished, each by the proper symbol of his patron-god impressed upon his *forehead*, but by a milder process than of old, being traced, not in his own blood, but with the ashes of cow-dung, the powder of sandal-wood, or coloured-earths, daily renewed. Inasmuch as amongst them the symbol of Fire (Bramah) is an equilateral Triangle, with the apex pointing upwards, it may be *conjectured* that the Mithraic χάραγμα was the same simple figure, by which indeed Horapollo informs us the Egyptians symbolised the Moon, and Plutarch that Pythagoras expressed the goddess Athene.* Clarkson, however, asserts positively that the Mark of Mithras was the " Tau mysticum," but whence he derived this knowledge I have never been able to ascertain.†

The *Seven Stars*, so conspicuous upon these talismans, doubtless stand for something higher than the mere planets; in all likelihood they denote the Seven Amshaspands, the First Order of Angels in the Zoroastrian hierarchy; and who became the " Seven Spirits of God " to the later Jews, and thence by gradual transition gave the epithet " Septiformis munere " to the Spiritus Sanctus of Christianity. Of these Amshaspands the names and offices are: Ormuzd, source of life and creation; Bahman, king of the world; Ardibehest, giver of fire; Shahrivar, of the metals; Çpandarmat (the Gnostic Sophia), queen of the earth; Khordad, presiding over time and the seasons; Amerdad, over trees and plants. Of these the highest in place are (after Ormuzd) the four named next in gradation. Below this order stand the Izeds, twenty-seven in number, ruled over by Mithras; they govern the heavenly bodies and the elements.

* Herself the lunar deity, according to an old tradition preserved by Aristotle.

† There is very good reason to discover a Mithraic mark in the " Phanaces " or, Sun between two Crescents, the regular badge of the kings of Pontus, and as such put upon the states of Athens bearing the names of Mithridates and Aristion. (In the Duc de Luynes Collection.)

Against each Amshaspand and Ized is arrayed a corresponding Angel of Darkness, to thwart all his operations, namely, the Seven Arch-Devs, and the Twenty-Seven Devs.

V. GNOSTIC SACRAMENTS AND INITIATIONS AS CONNECTED WITH THE MITHRAIC.

In my account of Mithraicism notice has been taken of the very prominent part that sacraments for the remission of sin play in the ceremonial of that religion; the following extracts from the grand Gnostic text-book will serve to show how the same notions (and probably, forms) were transferred to the service of Gnosticism.

Baptism, Remitting Sins.—(Pistis-Sophia) (298). Then came forth Mary and said : Lord, under what form do *Baptisms* remit sins ? I have heard thee saying that the Ministers of Contentions (ἐριδαῖοι)* follow after the soul, bearing witness against it of all the sins that it hath committed, so that they may convict it in the judgments. Now, therefore, Lord, do the mysteries of Baptism blot out the sins that be in the hands of the Receivers of Contention, so that they shall utterly forget the same ? Now, therefore, Lord, tell us in what form they remit sins; for we desire to know them thoroughly. Then the Saviour answered and said : Thou hast well spoken: of truth those Ministers are they that testify against all sins, for they abide constantly in the places of judgment, laying hold upon the souls, convicting all the souls of sinners who have not received the mystery, and they keep them fast in chaos tormenting them. But these contentious ones cannot pass over chaos so as to enter into the courses that be above chaos; in order to convict the souls therefore receiving the mysteries, it is not lawful for them to force so as to drag them down into chaos, where the Contentious Receivers may convict them. But the souls of such as have not received the mysteries, these do they desire and hail into chaos : whereas the souls that have received

* The Cabiri, " punishers," of the ancient mythology, performing their former duties under the new dispensation.

the mysteries, they have no means of convicting, seeing that they cannot get out of their own place; and even if they did come forth, they could not stop those souls, neither shut them up in their chaos. Hearken, therefore, I will declare to you in truth in what form the mystery of Baptism remitteth sins. If the souls when yet living in the world have been sinful, the Contentious Receivers verily do come, that they may bear witness of all the sins they have committed, but they can by no means come forth out of the regions of chaos, so as to convict the soul in the places of judgment that be beyond chaos. But the counterfeit of the spirit* testifies against all the sins of the soul, in order to convict it in the places of judgment that be beyond chaos; not only doth it testify, but also sets a *seal* upon all the sins of the soul, so as to print them firmly upon the soul, that all the Rulers of the judgment place of the sinners may know that it is the soul of a sinner, and likewise know the *number* of sins which it hath committed from the seals that the counterfeit of the spirit hath imprinted upon it, so that they may punish the soul according to the number of its sins: this is the manner in which they treat the soul of a sinner. (300). Now therefore if any one hath received the mysteries of Baptism, *those mysteries become a great fire,*† exceeding strong, and wise, so as to burn up all the sins: and the Fire entereth into the soul secretly, so that it may consume within it all the sins which the counterfeit of the spirit hath printed there. Likewise it entereth into the body secretly, that it may pursue all its pursuers, and divide them into parts—for it pursueth within the body, the counterfeit of the spirit, and Fate—so that it may divide them apart from the Power and the Soul, and place them in one part of the body—so that the fire separates the counterfeit of the spirit, Fate, and the Body into one portion, and the Soul and the Power ‡ into another portion. The mystery of Baptism remaineth in the middle of them, so that it may perpetually separate them, so that it may purge and cleanse them in order

---

* 'Αντιμῖμον Πνεύματος, one of the four component parts of the soul; equivalent apparently to our "Conscience."

† A clear allusion to the Mithraic "torture of the fire."

‡ The particle of the Godhead mixed up in the quadruple composi- of the Inner Man.

that they may not be polluted by *Matter*. Now therefore, Mary, this is the manner whereby the mystery of Baptism remitteth sins and all transgressions.

(301) And when the Saviour had thus spoken, he said to his disciples: Do ye understand in what manner I speak with you? Then came forth Mary, saying : Of a truth, Lord, I perceive in reality all the things that thou hast said. Touching this matter of the Remission of Sins, thou speaketh aforetime to us in a parable, saying: I am come to bring *fire* upon the earth; nay, more, let it burn as much as I please. And, again thou hast set it forth openly, saying: I have a baptism wherewith I will baptise and how shall I endure until it be accomplished? Ye think that I am come to bring peace upon the earth? By no means so, but dissension, which I am come to bring. For from this time forth there shall be five in one house; three shall be divided against two, and two against three. This, Lord, is the word that thou speakest openly. But concerning the word that thou spakest: I am come to bring fire upon the earth, and let it burn so much as I please: in this thou hast spoken of the mystery of Baptism in the world, and let it burn as much as thou pleasest for to consume all the sins of the soul, that it may purge them away. And again thou hast shewn the same forth openly, saying : I have a baptism wherewith I will baptise, and how shall I endure until it be accomplished? The which is this; Thou wilt not tarry in the world until the baptisms be accomplished to purify all the perfect souls. And again what thou spakest unto us aforetime: " Do ye suppose I am come to bring peace upon earth," &c. (302). This signifieth the mystery of Baptism which thou hast brought into the world, because it hath brought about dissension in the body of the world, because it hath divided the Counterfeit of the spirit, the Body, and the Fate thereof, into one party, and the Soul and the Power into the other party. The same is, " There shall be three against two, and two against three." And when Mary had spoken these things the Saviour said : Well done, thou Spiritual One in the pure light, this is the interpretation of my saying.

Then Mary went on and said : Bear with me, Lord, whilst I yet inquire of thee. Lo! we know now fully after what form

Baptism remitteth sin. Now therefore declare unto us the mystery of the Three Courts, and the mystery of the First Mystery, and likewise the mystery of the Ineffable One; in what form do these also remit sin? Do they remit sin in the *form of baptism* or not? (303) The Saviour answered again: By no means; but all the mysteries of the Three Courts remit in the soul, and in all the regions of the Rulers, all the sins that the soul hath committed even from the beginning. They remit also the sins that the soul shall have committed afterwards up to the time that each one of the mysteries taketh unto itself, the time whereof I will declare unto you hereafter. Moreover the mystery of the First Mystery, and the mystery of the Ineffable One, remit unto the soul in all the regions of the Rulers all the sins and transgressions that it hath committed. And not only do they remit, but they do not *impute sin** to the soul, from henceforth for ever by reason of the free-grace of the mystery and the exceeding glory of the same. Then said the Saviour: Do ye understand all that I have said unto you? Then Mary answered: Lord, I have caught up all the words thou hast spoken. Now therefore as to the saying that all the mysteries of the Three Courts remit sins, and blot out iniquities. Concerning this same matter hath David the prophet spoken, saying: "Blessed are they whose sins they have remitted, and whose iniquities they have covered," and as to thy saying that the mystery of the First Mystery, and the mystery of the Ineffable One, do not only remit all sin unto the soul for ever, but also do not suffer sin to be *imputed* unto the same for ever and ever, by reason of the free-gift of the great mystery, and the exceeding glory thereof; concerning this same matter David the prophet foretold, saying: "Blessed are they unto whom the Lord will not impute sin," which signifieth they will not impute sin from henceforth unto those that receive the mystery of the First Mystery and the mystery of the Ineffable One. Then answered the Saviour: Well done, thou Spiritual One, this is the interpretation of my word.

(305) Then Mary continued, saying: Lord, if a man shall

---

* This is the doctrine that "knowledge" renders all actions free from infulness—as held by the Simonians.

have received the mystery in the mystery of the First Mystery, and afterwards shall turn back and sin, and again shall repent and pray in his own mystery, shall his sin be remitted to him or not? Then answered the Saviour: Whosoever after receiving the mystery shall again sin twelve times, and again repent twelve times, and then shall pray in his own mystery, his sin shall be remitted unto him. But and if, after these twelve times, he shall turn again and transgress, then of a truth his sin shall never more be remitted, so that he may turn again unto his own mystery whatsoever it be. For such an one there is no repentance, unless indeed he hath received the mystery of the Ineffable One that remitteth all sins, and shall remit them at every time.

Then said Mary: Lord, those who have received the mystery of the First Mystery, and then have turned back and sinned, if such without having repented shall depart out of the body, shall they inherit the kingdom or not, forasmuch as they have received the free gift of that mystery? (306) The Saviour answered: Of such the judgment shall be the most merciful amongst all the judgments, for their dwelling is in the Middle Gate* of the Dragon of Outer Darkness, and at the end† of all those that be in torment: because such an one hath received the free gift of the mystery, and hath not remained stead-fast therein. Then said Mary: Such as have received the mystery of the Ineffable One and then shall turn back and sin, but afterwards shall repent in their lifetime, how many times shall their sin be remitted unto *them*? Then answered the Saviour: To such an one, not only if he turn back and sin once, and then repent, shall his sin be remitted, but even if he doth so continually, so long as he shall repent whilst yet alive, not being in hypocrisy, and shall pray according to his own mystery, because those mysteries are merciful and remit sin at every time (307). Then asked Mary: But if such an one shall depart out of the body before he hath repented, what then shall happen unto him? (307) Then answered the Saviour: Of such an one the judgment shall be worse than of any other, and

---

* This term is borrowed from the ancient Gates of the Amenti.

† The lost place, answering to the Limbo of the mediæval Hell.

exceeding great; for even if those souls be *new ones*,* they shall not return unto the changes of the earthly bodies, neither shall they do any work, but they shall be cast out into the uttermost parts of the Outer Darkness, and shall be consumed so that they shall not exist for ever and ever.

(308) To this declaration Mary refers the saying: "Salt is good, but if the salt hath lost its savour," &c.

The following extracts, from the same high authority, will much elucidate the *pass-words* communicated to the dying believer, which form so important a feature of the Gnostic system.

Benefits of Initiation.—I will declare unto you that mystery, which is this: Whosoever shall have received that *One Word*, when he shall depart out of the body of the Matter of the Rulers, there shall come the Contentious Receivers to loosen him out of that body, which same Receivers loosen every one departing out of the body. And when they shall have loosened the soul that hath received that mystery which I have declared unto you, in that very moment wherein he is set loose, he becometh a great *flood of light* in the midst of them. And the Receivers shall fear the light of that soul, and shall tremble, and shall cease through their fear of the great light which they behold. And that soul shall fly up aloft, and the Receivers shall not lay hold upon him, neither shall they discern by what way he is gone, inasmuch as he is become a great *Ray of Light*, and flieth up aloft, neither is there any Power that can overtake him, nor ever come nigh unto him at all (228). But he passes through all the regions of the Rulers, and also the regions of the offspring of the Light, neither doth he give-in a declaration in any region, nor yet a defence of himself,† nor yet the pass-word (or symbol). Neither can any Power of them all draw near him, but all the regions of the Rulers and of the offspring of the Light shall

* That is, have occupied the body for the first time; not souls that after punishment for their sins in this life, have been placed again in bodies to undergo a second probation upon earth.

† All this is borrowed from the Egyptian "Ritual of the Dead," concerning the soul's passage on its way to the palace of Osiris Socharis, "the Occidental," through the One-and-twenty *Gates*, each guarded by its own Genius, and each requiring a separate address.

sing hymns, each one in his own place, fearing the flood of light that clotheth that soul, until he shall come into the place of the heirs of the mystery that he hath received, and become conjoined with the members of the same. Verily, I say unto you, he shall be in all the regions in the time that a man can shoot an arrow. Again I say unto you, whosoever shall receive that mystery and make himself perfect in all the types and figures thereof, that man is in the world, but he is more excellent than the angels, and shall be before them all; he is a man in the world, but he is better than the archangels and shall be before them all (229); he is higher than all the tyrants, and all the lords, and all the gods, and all the luminaries, and all the pure ones, and all the triple powers, and all the Primal Fathers, and all the Unseen Ones; he is a man in the world, but he is more excellent than the great unseen Primal Father, and shall be more exalted than he, and above all those pertaining to the Middle-space, and above all the emanations of the Treasury of Light, and above all the confusion,* and above every region of the Treasure of Light; he is a man in the world, but he shall reign with me (230) in my kingdom; he is a man in the world, but he shall be a king in the Light; he is a man in the world, but he is not of the world; and verily I say unto you, that man is *I*, and I am *that man;* and in the dissolution of the world, when the universe shall be raised up, and all the number of perfect souls shall be raised up, and I am made king over all the offspring of the Light, and when I am made king over the seven AMHN,† and the Five Trees, and the Three AMHN, and the Nine Keepers; and when I am king over the Boy of the boy which be the Twin Saviours, and over the Twelve Saviours, and over all the number of perfect souls which have received the mystery of Light, then whosoever shall have received the mystery of the Ineffable One, they shall be joint kings with me and shall sit upon my right hand and upon my left hand in my kingdom. Verily I say unto you, those men are I, and I am

---

* The Creation of the Demiurgus, in which the Particle of the Godhead is *mixed up* and lost in the heap of Matter.

† Title probably borrowed from the former *Amenti,* the four sons of Osiris, and keepers of Elysium.

those men. For this cause have I said to you formerly, ye shall sit upon your thrones on my right hand and on my left in my kingdom, and ye shall reign together with me (231). Therefore I did not refrain, neither was I abashed to call you my brethren and my fellows, inasmuch as ye shall be joint kings with me in my kingdom. These things therefore I said unto you, knowing that I was about to give unto you the mystery of the Ineffable One, because that mystery is I, and I am that mystery. Now therefore not only ye shall reign with me, but also whatsoever men shall have received that mystery they shall be joint kings with me in my kingdom; and I am they, and they are I. But my throne shall be more exalted than theirs; and inasmuch as ye shall receive sorrows in this world beyond all other men whilst ye are preaching the words that I declare unto you, therefore your thrones shall be next to my throne in my kingdom. For this cause I said of old time, in the place where I shall be, my twelve ministers shall be also; but Mary Magdalene, and John the Virgin, shall be the most excellent amongst my disciples. And all men that shall have received the mystery of the Ineffable One shall be upon my right hand and upon my left, for I am they and they are I, and they shall be equal with you in every thing; but your thrones shall be more exalted than theirs, and my throne shall be more exalted than yours (232). And all men that shall find out the *Word* of the Ineffable One, verily I say unto you all the men that shall know that *Word*, the same shall understand also the knowledge of all the words that I have spoken unto you, both in their depth and in their height, in their length and in their breadth. And what things I have not told you those I will tell you in their place and in their order in the emanation of the universe. Verily I say unto you, they shall know how the world is established, and after what form those that pertain unto the height (highest place) be made, and for what end the universe was created.

And when the Saviour had said these things, Mary Magdalene came forward and said : Lord, be not wroth with me if I seek out everything with diligence. Whether is the Word of the mystery of the Ineffable One, one thing, and the Word of the Knowledge of All, another? Then the Saviour answered, and said: The Word of the mystery of the Ineffable is one thing, and the Word of the Knowledge of All is another. Then said Mary: Suffer me, Lord, to ask thee yet again one thing. Unless when we are living we understand the knowledge of the whole Word of the Ineffable One, we shall not inherit the kingdom of Light? (233). Then the Saviour answered, and said: Of a truth, whosoever shall have received the mystery of the kingdom of Light, the same shall go to inherit it into that place the mystery whereof he hath received. But he shall not obtain the knowledge of the All, wherefore all things were made, except he shall have known that One Word of the Ineffable, the which is the knowledge of all. And again, there is no way of knowing that One Word of knowledge, except a man shall have first received the mystery of the Ineffable One; but every man shall go to inherit that place the mystery whereof he hath received. For which cause I said to you formerly: " He that believeth a prophet shall receive a prophet's reward, and he that believeth a righteous man shall receive a righteous man's reward," which is this: of whatsoever place each hath received the mystery, into that same place shall he go. He that hath received a humble mystery, the same shall inherit a humble place. He that hath received an excellent mystery, the same shall inherit an exalted place; and every one shall abide in his own place in the light of my kingdom, and every one shall have authority over the Course that is below him, but over that which is above himself he shall not have authority, but shall abide in his inheritance of the light of my kingdom, dwelling in a great light unto which there is no measure, next to the gods and to the Unseen Ones, and he shall be in great joy and gladness (234).

Now therefore I will speak with you touching the glory of those also that shall receive the mystery of the First Mystery. He that hath received the same, at the time when he shall depart out of this body of Matter, the Contentious Receiver shall come that they may take his soul out of the body, and that soul shall become a great Ray of light and shall fly aloft through the midst of them, and shall pass through all the regions and shall not give-in any declaration, or defence, or symbol, token (pass-word), but shall pass through all, that he may come and reign over all the places belonging to the First Saviour. In the like manner he that hath received the Second Mystery and the Third and Fourth up to the Twelfth* (235), that soul likewise shall pass through all the regions without giving in his defence, or token, and shall come and reign over all the places belonging to the Twelve Saviours. And in like manner those receiving the second mystery shall reign over the places of the Second Saviour amongst the heirs of light. In like manner those receiving the third and the fourth up to the twelfth, shall reign over the regions of that Saviour whose mystery each hath received. But they shall not be equal with those that have received the mystery of the Ineffable One, but shall abide in the Courses of the Twelve Saviours.

Then Mary answered, saying: Lord, suffer me yet again. How is it that the First Mystery hath twelve mysteries, whereas the Ineffable hath but one? Jesus answered: Of a truth He hath but One, but that mystery maketh *three* others; the mystery is indeed *one*, but to each of them there is a different form, and moreover it maketh *five* mysteries.

As for the First Mystery, when thou hast performed it well in all the forms thereof, when thou departest out of thy body thou shalt forthwith become a great Ray of light, and it shall traverse all the regions of the Rulers and all the regions of Light, all being afraid of that light of the soul, until it shall come into its own kingdom. As for the Second Mystery, he that shall perform the same rightly in all the forms thereof, if he speak it over the head of a man departing out of the body, and *into his two ears*, that man departing out of the body when he hath received the mystery a second time, and been made partaker of the *Word of Truth,*† that man's soul shall become, when it leaveth the body, a great flood of light, so as to traverse all the regions until it cometh into the kingdom of that mystery. But and if

---

* This gradation seems borrowed from the twelve degrees in the Mithraic initiation.

† This is what Epiphanius relates of the practice of the Heracleonites of communicating the pass-word to the ear of the dying man.

that man hath not received that mystery, neither hath been made partaker of the words of truth, if he that hath performed that mystery shall speak the same into the ears of him who is departing out of the body, verily I say unto you, the soul of that man, although he hath not received the mystery of Light nor partaken of the words of truth, shall not be judged in the places of the Rulers, neither shall it be punished in any place, neither shall the fire touch it, by reason of the mystery of the Ineffable which goeth along with it. And they shall hasten to deliver that soul one to the other, and shall guide it Course after Course, and place (239) after place, until they bring it before the Virgin of Light: for all the regions shall fear the mystery and the *Mark** of the kingdom of the Ineffable One that is with it.

And when they have brought the soul unto the Virgin of Light, she shall see the Mark of the mystery of the kingdom of the Ineffable One which is with it. And the Virgin of Light marvelleth thereat, and she judgeth that soul, but suffereth him not to be brought unto the light until he hath accomplished the ministry of the light of that mystery, which be these: the purification of the renouncing of the world and of all the *Matter* that therein is. And the Virgin of Light sealeth him with a special seal, which is this: in the same month in which he hath departed out of the body, she will cause him to be placed in another body that shall be righteous, and shall obtain the divinity of truth and the high mystery, so that he may inherit the same, and also inherit the Light for ever and ever. This is the grace of the Second Mystery of the Ineffable One.

As touching the Third Mystery: the man that hath performed the same duly in all the forms thereof and shall *name* that mystery over the head of one departing out of the body whether he be living or *dead, or abiding in the midst of the torments of the Rulers,†* and their different fires, they shall make haste to release

---

* It has the impression of the royal seal stamped upon it.

† Here we have the first hint of masses performed for the dead. A similar idea is involved in the practice mentioned by St. Paul of being "baptized for the sake of deceased persons." A singular Italian usage alluded to by Dante in his 'Vendetta di Dio non Teme Suppe,' refers to something of the sort done to appease the manes. A homicide who had eaten sops in wine upon the grave of the slain man was thereby freed from the *vendetta* of the family.—(Purgat. xxxiii. 35.)

that man out of them all, and shall bring him before the Virgin of Light, who shall place him in a righteous body that shall inherit the light.

(243) Moreover in the dissolution of the Universe, that is, when the number of perfect souls is made up, and the mystery is accomplished on account of which the Universe has been created, then I will spend a thousand years, according to the years of light, ruling over the offspring of the light, and over the number of the perfect souls which have received all the mysteries. Then Mary said, Lord, how many years in the years of this world is one year of light? Jesus answered, One day of light is one thousand years of this world, wherefore thirty and six myriads and a half of the years of the world make one year of light. I shall therefore reign a thousand years of light, being king in the middle of the last *Parastates*,* being king over all the offspring of light, and over all the number of perfect souls that have received the mysteries of light. And ye, my disciples, and each one that hath received the mysteries of the Ineffable One, shall be upon my right hand and upon my left, being kings together with me in my kingdom. And those likewise that receive the three mysteries of the five mysteries of the Ineffable shall be kings together with you in the kingdom of light. But they shall not be equal with you, and with those receiving the mystery of the Ineffable One, for they shall continue kings behind you. And those receiving the five mysteries of the Ineffable shall remain behind the three mysteries being kings also. Likewise those receiving the twelve mysteries of the First Mystery, they too shall abide as kings behind the five mysteries of the Ineffable One. And they also are kings each one of them according to his course, and all receiving in the mysteries in all the places of the Court of the Ineffable One, so that they shall be kings also but come after such as have received the mystery of the First Mystery : being sent forth according to the glory of each, so that those receiving high mysteries shall dwell in high places, but those receiving humble mysteries shall abide in humble places.

* The deity whose place is next to the Supreme Light; to judge from the primary sense of the word.

These are the *Three Lots* of the Kingdom of Light, and the mysteries of these Three Lots of Light are exceeding great. Ye will find them in the great Second Book of IEV; but I will give unto you and declare unto you the mysteries of each lot, which be more exalted than any other place (246), and are chief both as to place and as to order: the which also lead all mankind within, into lofty places; according to the court belonging to their inheritance, so that ye have no need of any of the *lower mysteries*, but ye will find them in the Second Book of IEV which Enoch wrote when I spoke with him out of the Tree of Knowledge and out of the Tree of Life in the Paradise of Adam.

Now therefore after I shall have declared unto you all Emanation, I will give and I will tell unto you the Three Lots of my Kingdom which be the chief of all.

Inasmuch as *Ordeals* and *Meritorious Penances* held so important a place in the Mithraic ceremonial, it will not be irrelevant here to adduce for comparison a series of the kind as excogitated by the extravagant imagination of the Brahmins. The penances of the *demon* Taraka, the Tapa-asura, by means whereof he constrained Brahma to grant him whatever he chose to demand, are thus enumerated, each stage being of one century's duration. 1. He stood on one foot, holding up the other with both hands towards heaven, his eyes fixed immovably upon the sun. 2. He stood on one great toe. 3. He took for sustenance nothing but water. 4. He lived similarly upon air. 5. He remained immersed in the water. 6. He was buried in the earth, continuing, as during the last penance, in continued adoration. 7. He performed the same act in the fire. 8. He stood on his head with his feet upwards. 9. He stood resting on one hand. 10. He hung by his hands from a tree. 11. He hung on a tree by his feet, with his head downwards. (The twelfth degree Moor has, for some reason, omitted.)

By means like these, termed the *Yog*, the ascetic *Yogi* is enabled to obtain nine several gifts, that set him above all the laws of Nature. For example, he may expand or contract his body to any size he pleases; he may float in the air upon a sunbeam; he may exert all his sense at an infinite distance from the objects of them; with other capabilities of like kind.

And with respect to the sixth penance of Taraka, this, incredible as it appears, is still performed. To be buried alive in a small vault covered deep with earth until a crop of grain, sown over him at the time of inhumation, shall be ripe for cutting, is yet esteemed the most efficacious of good works for extorting from heaven the blessing most desired by the patient or his *employer* (the doctrine of *vicarious* atonement being most thoroughly Hindoo). The English Resident at Runjeet Singh's court has minutely described all the preparation made by the royal proxy, (whose regular trade it was thus to die for others), and the successful completion of his penance, which occupied the space of six weeks. The Resident assisted at the closing and the opening of the vault, and was certain that no deception could possibly have been practised by the Yogi. The blessing aimed at was the gift of fecundity for a favourite queen of Runjeet's.

The "Taurobolia," or *Baptism of Blood*, during the later ages of the Western Empire, held the foremost place, as the means of purification from sin, however atrocious. Prudentius has left a minute description of this horrid rite, in which the person to be regenerated, being stripped of his clothing, descended into a pit, which was covered with planks pierced full of holes; a bull was slaughtered upon them, whose hot blood, streaming down through these apertures (after the fashion of a shower-bath), thoroughly drenched the recipient below. The selection of the particular victim proves this ceremony in connection with the Mithraica, which latter, as Justin says, had a "Baptism for the remission of Sins"; and the Bull being in that religion the recognised emblem of *life*, his blood necessarily constituted the most effectual laver of regeneration. No more conclusive evidence of the value then attached to the Taurobolia can be adduced, than the fact mentioned by Lampridius that the priest-emperor Heliogabalus thought it necessary to submit to its performance; and a pit, constructed for the purpose as late as the fourth century, has lately been discovered within the sacred precincts of the Temple at Eleusis, the most holy spot in all Greece.

The subject will find its most appropriate conclusion in the

list of "Degrees" to be taken in the Mysteries, as laid down by
M. Lajard, in his elaborate treatise, 'Le Culte de Mithra,'*
These degrees were divided into four stages, Terrestrial, Aerial,
Igneous, and Divine, each consisting of three. The Terrestrial
comprised the Soldier, the Lion, the Bull. The Aerial, the
Vulture, the Ostrich, the Raven. The Igneous, the Gryphon,
the Horse, the Sun. The Divine, the Eagle, the Sparrow-Hawk,
the Father of fathers. Lajard's theory is best elucidated by
quoting his way of expounding a very frequent cylinder-subject.
He finds the admission to the degree of "The Soldier," in the
group where a man is seen standing before a "hierophant," or
priest, who stands on the back of a bull *couchant* on a platform.
The hierophant, wearing a cap tipped by a crescent, holds out
to the neophyte a curved sword, symbol of admission into the
Order. A priestess stands apart, separated from him by the
horn, or Tree of Life, over which soars the emblem of the
Assyrian Triad. Her cap is tipped by the Sun-star, but she
also wears the crescent, to show the hermaphrodite nature of
Mylitta!

* Lajard discovers upon the Baby-lonian cylinders representations of admission to the several degrees, of which they were given, as certificate to the initiated : and accounts for their enormous extant numbers by the supposition that every one, upon proceeding to a higher degree, threw away the cylinder marking the pre-ceding one. But the complicated system of the Mithraici was evi-dently the creation of much later times, and of a religion vainly strug-gling for life.

Fig 5

ST. AUGUSTINE ON GNOSTICISM.

The transition from orthodoxy to Gnosticism, in its last and most elaborate phase is well pointed out by the following reminiscences of St. Augustine, describing his own experiences. In his eighteenth or nineteenth year he had begun to study the Scriptures, to satisfy himself as to the truth of the religion in which he had been brought up. " Consequently I set to work to study the Holy Scriptures, in order that I might discover what was their true character. And lo! I behold a thing not discovered unto the proud, nor revealed unto babes; but humble in gait, lofty in issue, and veiled in mysteries; and I was not such a one as could enter therein, neither to bow down my neck unto the steps thereof. For I did not think then, as I speak *now*, when I was studying Scripture, but it seemed to me unworthy to be compared with the sublimity of Cicero's eloquence. Nevertheless that Scripture was such as should grow up together with babes, but I disdained to be a babe, and being puffed up with pride I fancied myself a grown-up man. So it came to pass that I fell in with men full of pride, dotards, too carnal, and great talkers, in whose mouth is a snare of the Devil, and bird-lime made up with a mixture of the syllables of Thy Name, and of our Lord Jesus Christ, and of the Paraclete's, our Comforter the Holy Ghost. All these names did not proceed out of their mouth except as far as the sound and echo of the tongue go, but their heart was utterly void of truth. And they used to repeat ' Truth and Truth,' and so did they repeat her name to me, but she was nowhere amongst them, but they spoke false things, not only concerning thee who art the Truth in truth, but even concerning the elements of this world of ours, thy creation; concerning which even the philosophers, who declared what is true, I ought to have slighted for the love of Thee, O my Father, the Supreme Good, the Beauty of all things beautiful. O Truth! Truth! how inwardly did the marrow of my soul sigh after thee even then, whilst *they* were

perpetually dinning thy name into my ears, and after various
fashions with the mere voice, and with *many and huge books* of
theirs.   And these were the dishes upon which were served up
to me who was hungering after thee, nothing but the *Sun and
the Moon*, thy fair works indeed, but not thyself, and not even
the *first* amongst thy works.   For thy spiritual works are
before those corporeal works, however splendid and heavenly
they may be.   But even for those, thy higher works, I hungered
and thirsted not, but for thee only, O Truth! wherein there is
no change, neither shadow of turning.   And again there were
set before me, in those same dishes, splendid phantoms, than
which it were even better to love the Sun himself, for *he* was
true as far as regards one's eyes, rather than to love those
fictions whereby the soul was deceived through the eyes.   And
yet because I believed them to be Thee, I ate thereof though not
greedily, because Thou didst not taste in my mouth as thou
really art, for thou wert not those empty fictions; neither
was I nourished thereby, but rather weakened.   Food in dreams
is like to the food of one awake, yet the sleepers are not fed by
the same, for they sleep on: but those dishes were not in any
wise like unto Thee as thou *now* hast spoken to me, &c."

Fig. 6.

THE WORSHIP OF SERAPIS.

I. THE FIGURED REPRESENTATIONS OF SERAPIS.

The next great series of monuments to be considered are those emanating from the worship of Serapis, that mysterious deity, who, under his varying forms, had, during the second and third centuries of our era, completely usurped the sovereignty of his brother Jupiter, and reduced him to the rank of a mere planetary Genius. Unlike the generality of the deities who figure upon the Gnostic stones, the *Alexandrian* Serapis does not belong to the primitive mythology of Egypt.* His worship may be said to be only coeval with the rise of Alexandria, into which city it was introduced from Sinope by the first Ptolemy, in consequence of the command (and repeated threats, in case of neglect) of a vision which had appeared to him. After three years of ineffectual negotiation, Ptolemy at last obtained the god from Scythotherius, king of Sinope; but when the citizens still refused to part with their idol, a report was spread, that it had spontaneously found its way from the temple down to the Egyptian ships lying in the harbour.

The prevalent opinion amongst the Greeks was that the figure represented Jupiter *Dis* (Aidoneus) and the one by his side, *Proserpine.* This latter the envoys were ordered by the same divine messenger, to leave in its native shrine. Another story, also mentioned by Tacitus,† made the statue to have been brought from Seleucia by Ptolemy III, but this rested on slighter authority. It is, however, a curious confirmation of this last tradition that Serapis is named by Plutarch ("Alexander,") as the chief deity of *Babylon* (Seleucia in later times) at the date of the Macedonian Conquest—a proof that

---

* The difference between him and the ancient Theban Serapis (as the Greeks translated his title "Osor-Api"), shall be pointed out farther on.

† Who narrates the whole affair at great length—a proof of the influence of the religion in his day—in his History, iv. 84.

he at least regarded that god as identical with *Belus*. Now, it
is a remarkable coincidence that *Ana*, the First Person in the
primitive Chaldean Triad, is likewise " King of the Lower
World," and that his symbol, the vertical wedge, stands also for
the numeral 60, which last is often used to express hiero-
glyphically the name Ana.

It was Timotheus, an Athenian Eumolpid, and, in virtue of
his descent, Diviner to the king, who indicated Pontus as the
residence of the unknown god, whose apparition had so dis-
quieted the monarch by commanding himself to be sent for
without declaring whence.   The figure, seen in the vision, was
that of a *youth*, a circumstance that tallies ill with the mature
majesty of the great god of Alexandria.*   But the Helios
Dionysos, a veritable Chrishna, who graces the reverse of the
gold medallion of Pharnaces II, coined at Sinope in the following century, agrees much more exactly with this description of
the nocturnal visitor.

Speedily did Serapis become the sole lord of his new home ;
and speculations as to his true nature employed the ingenuity
of the philosophers at Alexandria, down to the times when
they were superseded by the discussions on the doctrine of
the Trinity, waged with equal zeal but infinitely worse temper.
Every conflicting religion strove to claim him as the grand
representative of their own doctrine.   Macrobius has preserved one of the most ingenious of these interpretations, as
made by the ' Rationalists,' a party so strong amongst the later
Greeks (I. 20).   " The City of Alexandria pays an almost
frantic worship to Serapis and Isis, nevertheless they show that
all this veneration is merely offered to the *Sun* under that name,
both by their placing the corn-measure upon his head, and by
accompanying his statue with the figure of an animal having
three heads ; of these heads, the middle and the largest one is a

---

* The great god of Assyria, Adad,
"The One," the oracle-giving Jupiter
of Heliopolis, was thus figured in
his *golden* statue as a beardless
youth, brandishing aloft a whip, and
holding in his left hand the thunderbolt and wheat-ears. The rays crown-
ing his head pointed downwards to
signify their influence upon the earth,
who stood before him in the figure of
Atergatis, the rays in her crown
pointing upwards, to express the
springing up of her gifts. She was
supported, like Cybele, upon the
backs of lions.

lion's, that which rises on the right is a dog's in a peaceable and fawning attitude; whilst the left part of the neck terminates in that of a ravening wolf. All these bestial forms are connected together by the wreathed body of a serpent, which raises its head up towards the god's right hand, on which side the monster is placed. The *lion's* head typifies the Present, because its condition between the Past and the Future is strong and fervent. The Past is signified by the *wolf's* head, because the memory of all things past is scratched away from us and utterly consumed. The emblem of the fawning *dog* represents the Future, the domain of inconstant and flattering hope. But whom should Past, Present and Future serve except their Authors? His head crowned with the *calathus* typifies the *height* of the planet above us, also his all-powerful *capaciousness*, since unto him all things earthly do return, being drawn up by the heat he emits. Moreover when Nicocreon, tyrant of Cyprus, consulted Serapis as to which of the gods he ought to be accounted, he received the following response :—

> " ' A god I am, such as I show to thee,
> The starry heavens my head; my trunk the sea;
> Earth forms my feet; mine ears the air supplies;
> The sun's far-darting, brilliant rays mine eyes.' " *

From all this it is evident that the nature of Serapis and the Sun is one and indivisible. Again, Isis is universally worshipped as the type of earth, or Nature in subjection to the Sun. For this cause the body of the goddess is covered with continuous rows of *udders*, to declare that the universe is maintained by the perpetual nourishing of the Earth or Nature." This last curious remark shows that Macrobius regarded the Alexandrian Isis as the same with the Ephesian Diana, for the ancient Isis of Egypt had only the usual complement of breasts. This philosopher had started with the axiom (I. 17), " Omnes deos referri ad Solem," and begins by demonstrating from the various epithets

---

* I cannot help suspecting that this description supplied Basilides with the idea of his celebrated *Pantheus*, the Abraxas-figure. The head of the *bird* was the fittest emblem of the air, the *serpent*, according to Herodotus, was the offspring of earth, the *breast* of man was the Homeric attribute of Neptune.

of Apollo, that *he* was the same god with the one styled the Sun. He then proceeds to prove the same of Bacchus, Hermes, Aesculapius, and Hercules. His ingenious explanation of the serpent-entwined rod of Hermes, and club of Aesculapius, will be found applied further on to the elucidation of the remarkable symbol on the reverse of all the Chnuphis amulets. After this, Macrobius passes in review the attributes and legends of Adonis and Atys, also of Osiris and Horus, and comes to the same conclusion concerning the real nature of all these personages, adding parenthetically a very fanciful exposition of the Signs of the Zodiac, as being merely so many emblems of the solar influence in the several regions of creation. Nemesis, Paris, Saturn, Jupiter, and finally the Assyrian Adad, are all reduced by him to the same signification.

This brings us to that most wondrous identification of all, which Hadrian mentions in a letter to his brother-in-law Servianus, preserved by the historian Vopiscus in his Life of the Tyrant Saturninus. " Those who worship Serapis are likewise Christians ; even those who style themselves the bishops of Christ are devoted to Serapis. The very Patriarch himself,* when he comes to Egypt, is forced by some to adore Serapis, by others to worship Christ. There is but one God for them all, Him do the Christians, Him do the Jews, Him do the Gentiles, all alike worship." Severus Alexander, too, who daily paid his devotions to Christ and Abraham, did none the less expend large sums in decorating the temples of Serapis and Isis " with statues, *couches*, and all things pertaining to their Mysteries,"† whilst he left the other gods of Rome to take care of themselves.

And as connected with the same subject, it may be here observed that the conventional portrait of the Saviour is in all probability borrowed from the head of Serapis, so full of grave and pensive majesty. Of the first converts, the Jewish foredilections were so powerful that we may be sure that no attempt was made to portray His countenance until many generations

---

* The Patriarch of Tiberias, head of the Jewish religion, after the destruction of Jerusalem.

† A very favourite representation of Isis upon our talismans shows her reclining upon a couch.

M

after all who had beheld it on earth had passed away.* Nevertheless, the importance so long attached to the pretended letter of Lentulus to the emperor, Tiberius, describing Christ's personal appearance, demands a notice in this place. Its monkish Latinity and style betray it, at first sight, for the authorship of some mediæval divine. Yet, incredible as it may seem, even a learned man like Grynæus has been so besotted through his pious longing for the *reality* of such a record, as to persuade himself that Lentulus, a Roman Senator and an eminent historian, could have written in the exact phrase of a mendicant friar. "There has appeared in our times, and still lives, a Man of great virtue, named Christ Jesus, who is called by the Gentiles a Prophet of Truth, but whom his own disciples called the Son of God; raising the dead, and healing diseases. A man indeed of lofty stature, handsome, having a venerable countenance, which the beholders can both love and fear. His hair verily somewhat wavy and curling, somewhat brightish and resplendent in colour, flowing down upon his shoulders, having a parting in the middle of the head after the fashion of the Nazarenes, &c." (Grynæus, 'Orthodoxia' I. p. 2.) This forgery reminds one of Pliny's remark, "Pariunt desideria non traditos vultus, sicutin Homero evenit." The wish is father to the image of the venerated object; and the conception is too joyfully accepted by the loving soul for it to trouble itself overmuch in scrutinizing the legitimacy of the same: for, as Martial exclaims with full truth " quis enim damnet sua vota libenter?"

But to return to the Egypt of the times of Gnosticism. In the very focus of that theosophy, Alexandria, the syncretistic sects which sprang up so rankly there during the three first centuries of the Roman empire, had good grounds for making out Serapis a prototype of Christ, considered as Lord and Maker of all, and Judge of the quick and the dead. For the response given to Nicocreon, above quoted, evinces that the philosophers at least saw in Serapis nothing more than the emblem of the 'Anima

* What proves the want of any real authority for the portraits of the Saviour is the fact that the earliest monuments in sculpture or painting, represent him as *youthful* and *beardless*.

Mundi,' the *Spirit* of whom Nature universal is the *body*, for they held the doctrine of

" . . . . . . the one harmonious whole,
    Whose body Nature is, and God the soul."

So that by an easy transition Serapis came to be worshipped as the embodiment of the One Supreme, whose representative on earth was Christ.

The very *construction* of the grand Colossus of Serapis ingeniously set forth these ideas of his character. It was formed out of plates of *all the metals*, artfully joined together, to typify the harmonious union of different elements in the fabric of the universe, the " moles et machina mundi." This statue was placed upon the summit of an artificial hill (whose vast interior was divided into vaulted halls, containing the famous library), ascended by a flight of a hundred steps—a style of building totally diverse from the native Egyptian and the Grecian model, but exactly following the Indian usage, as may be seen by the grand pagoda of Siva at Tanjore, and by the *topes* and *dagobas* of the Buddhists.

The remarkable construction of this Colossus may reasonably be supposed to have suggested to the Alexandrian Jew, who completed the Book of Daniel, the notion of the similarly compacted *Image* which figures in Nebuchadnezzar's Dream. That his description of the latter was penned long after the coming of Serapis into that city is manifest from the minute details his *prophet* gives concerning the constant squabbles going on between Antiochus Epiphanes and Ptolemy Philometor, his nephew ; together with the final intervention of the Roman Senate. The popular belief of the Alexandrians (Christian as well as pagan) was that the profanation of this statue would be the signal for heaven and earth to collapse at once into pristine chaos—a notion bearing clear testimony to the grand idea embodied by the figure. At last, however, although his worship, thus defended by deep-rooted fear, had been tolerated by the Christian government long after the other gods of Egypt had been swept away, this wonderful Colossus was broken down by " that perpetual enemy of peace and virtue " the

Patriarch Theophilus, in the reign of Theodosius; and its mutilated trunk, dragged triumphantly through the streets by the mob of rejoicing fanatics, was ultimately buried in the Hippodrome.

Like that of Mithras, the worship of Serapis was widely diffused over the West. A very curious exemplification of this is to be found in Ammianus' notice that Mederich, king of the Alemanni, had, when detained as a hostage in Gaul, been taught certain Greek Mysteries, and for that reason changed the name of his son Aganerich into *Serapion.* But Serapis had a natural claim to the adoration of the Gauls, who, as Cæsar tells us, actually boasted of descent from *Dis Pater.*

The new-comer from Sinope does not seem to have brought his name with him. When Ptolemy consulted his own priesthood upon this important point, Manetho boldly identified the Pontic god with their own Osor-Apis, chiefly on the score of his attribute Cerberus, which he considered the counterpart of the hippopotamus-headed Typhon who attends Osor-Apis in his character of sovereign of the Lower World. This deity is no other than the Bull Apis, who, after death, assumes the figure of Osiris, the regular form of Egyptian apotheosis, and so frequently seen applied to deceased kings. Osor-Apis, as he now becomes, is depicted as a man with the head of a bull, and carrying the ensigns by which we usually recognize Osiris. The god of Alexandria therefore differs in form as widely as in origin from the original patron of Thebes, with whom he has no other affinity than in name, and *that* rests only on the arbitrary interpretation of the Egyptian priests, so successful in persuading the Greeks that the mythology of the whole world was but a plagiarism from their own.

M. Mariette in 1860 excavated the Theban Serapeum, as it was called in Roman times, with its long avenue of sphinxes; he also discovered the catacombs where the Apis Bulls were deposited after death, and found there no fewer than sixty, two of their mummies yet reposing undisturbed. It is amusing to notice how neatly the Greeks turned the Coptic Osor-Apis into the more euphonious ὁ Σάραπις.

II. THE PROBABLE ORIGIN OF SERAPIS.

The ancient speculations cited in the preceding chapter are all baseless theories, due to the ingenious refinements of the Alexandrian literati, and springing out of the system of allegorical interpretation in which the New Platonists so much delighted. It is evident that upon his *first introduction* into Egypt, Serapis was regarded by the Alexandrians as identical with Aïdoneus, or Dis, the Lord of the Lower World. Now, all his attributes suggest him to have been of *Indian* origin, and no other than *Yama*, "Lord of Hell," attended by his dog "Çarbara," *the spotted*, who has the epithet "Triçira," *three-headed*, and by his serpent "Çesha," called "Regent of Hades;" in fact, some have discovered in the name Serapis* but the Grecian form of Yama's epithet, "Sraddha-deva," *Lord of the obsequies*, that is, of the funeral sacrifices offered to the *Pitris* or *Manes*. Yama also is styled "Lord of souls," and "Judge of the dead;" another office assimilating him to Serapis in the character under which the latter came to be specially regarded —a point, moreover, which at a later date afforded stronger reasons for identifying him with Christ. A plausible etymology of the name Serapis may be found in another of Yama's epithets, "Asrik-pa" the *Blood-drinker*. This explanation is confirmed to some extent by the ancient tradition, of which Homer makes such fine use when he describes Ulysses' mode of evoking the ghosts, and their eagerness to lap up the life-blood of the victim (Od. xi. 35) :—

> "Seizing the victim sheep I pierced their throats;
> Flowed the black blood, and filled the hollow trench;
> Then from the abyss, eager their thirst to slake,
> Came swarming up the spirits of the dead."

And connected with the same notion was the practice of strewing *roses* over the graves of departed friends—

> "Purpureos spargam flores et fungar inani munere,"

for (as Servius explains it) the *red* colour of the flower

---

* It is not improbable that the name under which the god was worshipped at *Sinope* had something of this sound; and which suggested to Manetho the idea of identifying him with his own Osor-Api.

represented *blood*, and thereby served as a substitute for the living victim.*

This analogy between Yama and Serapis may be further extended by the consideration of certain other points connected with the office of the former deity. For example, unto the souls of the righteous he appears as "Dharma-rāja," and has a servant "Karma-la" (the Hermes Psychopompos of the Greeks), who brings them into his presence upon a self-moving car. But unto the wicked he is "Yama," and has for *them* another minister, "Kash-Mala," who drags them before him with halters round their necks, over rough and stony places. Other titles of Yama are "Kritānta" and "Mrityu." The connection of the latter with *Mors* is evident enough, making it a fitting appellation for *Dis* (*Ditis*), in which again unmistakably lies the root of our name *Death*, applied to the same Principle of Destruction.

Yama as "Sraddha-deva," monarch of "Pātāla" (the infernal regions), has for consort Bhavani, who hence takes the title of "Patala-devi," as upon Earth she is "Bhu-devi," in heaven, "Swardevi." Her lord owns, besides Çarbara, another dog named "Çyama," the *Black One* (now we see wherefore the mediæval familiar spirits like Cornelius Agrippa's black spaniel, and Faustus' "pudel" chose that particular figure), whom he employs as the minister of his vengeance. As Judge of Souls he displays two faces, the one benign, the other terrific. Another of his titles is "Kalantika," *Time as the Destroyer*: it can hardly be a mere accidental coincidence that such was the exact name given to the head-dress worn by the Egyptian priests when officiating—in later times a purple cloth covering the head, and falling down upon the neck, surmounted by two plumes.

* One of the most frequented places of pilgrimage at Benares is the "Gyan Bapi," "Well of Knowledge," in the depths whereof Siva himself resides. It was dug by the genius Rishi, with that god's own trident, to relieve the world after a twelve years' drought. The pilgrims throw into it offerings of all kinds, flowers included. Another well in the same city, of supreme efficacy for the washing away of all sin, is the *Manikarnika*, so called from the earring of Mahadeva, which fell into it. Vishnu had dug this well with his *changra*, quoit, and filled it with the luminous sweat of his body.

"Kali-Bhavani," the Destructive Female Principle is represented* in this character with a visage exactly identical with the most ancient type of the Grecian Gorgon—such as we still behold it guarding the Etruscan sepulchres, and lowering horrifically upon the sacrilegious intruder; as in that notable example in the tomb of the Volumni at Perugia, where it forms the centrepiece of the ceiling of the grand hall. Formed of a Tiger's head in its first conception by the excited fancy of Hindoo superstition, the Etruscan demon still exhibits the same protruded tongue, huge tusks, glaring eyes, wings in the hair, and serpents twining about the throat. Of such aspect was doubtless that "Gorgon's Head, the work of the Cyclops," which was shown to Pausanias as the most notable object in the Argive Acropolis—a proof that the earliest essays of Pelasgic art had been made in realising this idea. Again, in that most ancient monument of Grecian art, the Coffer of Cypselus (made before B.C. 600), the same traveller states (v. 19.), " Behind Polynices stands a female figure, having tusks as savage as those of a wild beast, and the nails of her fingers like unto talons: the inscription above her, *they tell you* means Κὴρ (Fate)." This name therefore must have been a *foreign* word, translated to Pausanias by the Custodian of the Temple. Plutarch (Life of Aratus) supplies another singular illustration of the Worship of these terrific idols of the olden time in the most polished ages of Greece. The Artemis of Pellene was of so dreadful an aspect that none dared to look upon her: and when carried in procession, her sight blasted the very tree and crops as she passed. When the Ætolians were actually in possession of and plundering the town, her priestess, by bringing this image out from the shrine, struck them with such terror that they made a precipitate retreat. This Artemis consequently must have been a veritable Hecate, a true Queen of Hell, an idol moreover of *wood*, ξόανον (like her of Ephesus), otherwise the priestess had not been able to wield it so effectually to scare away the marauders. Again, the recorded dream of Cimon, which presaged his death, was that a black bitch bayed

* Roth. 'Zeitschrift der Morgenländischen Gesellschaft,' iv. p. 425, and Mure in Royal Asiatic Society's Journal, i. p. 287.

at him in a half-human voice, " Come to me ; I and my whelps will receive thee gladly." The Hellenic gods, now and then shew themselves under an aspect strangely at variance with their usual benevolent and *jovial* character. A true Siva was that "Dionysos Omestes" (The Cannibal), unto whom Themistocles, forced by the Diviners, sacrificed the three sons of Sandauce, own sister to Xerxes, when taken prisoners on the eve of the Battle of Salamis. It must be remembered that tradition made Perseus bring back the Gorgon's Head, trophy of his success, from Ethiopia, a synonym at first for the remotest East—it being only in Roman times that " Ethiopia " was restricted to a single province of Africa. The *harpe* too, the weapon lent to the hero by Hermes, is from its form no other than the ankuṣa, elephant-hook, which is carried for attribute by so many of the Hindoo Deities.* Sufficient explanation this why Persephone (*Destroying-slayer*) was assigned by the earliest Greeks as Consort to Aidoneus ; and also why Ulysses, on his visit to her realms, should have been alarmed,

> " Lest from deep Hell Persephone the dread
> Should send the terror of the Gorgon's Head."

From the influence of this terror upon the otherwise undaunted wanderer, these same two lines came to be considered as endued with a wonderfully strong repellent power, for Marcellus Empiricus prescribes them to be whispered into the ear of any one choking from a bone or other matter sticking in his throat; or else to write them out on a paper to be tied around his throat, " Which will be equally effectual."

Lucian remarks (' Philopatris,') that the reason why the ancient warriors bore the Gorgon's Head upon their shields was because it served for an amulet against dangers of every sort; on the same account, in all likelihood, was it put for device on many archaic coinages; Populonia, Paros, &c. For

* The Gorgon of the gems (' Ant. Gems,' Pl. XX., 4), and of the coin of Neapolis is regularly to be seen, to this day, sculptured in relief upon the pillar set up on each side of the gates of Hindoo temples, as I am informed by our great oriental archæologist, Col. Pearse. She goes by the name of " Keeper of the Gate." Now we see why her head decorated the pediments of temples in Greece and Rome, and formed the keystone of triumphal arches even in the time of Constantine, as the lately-discovered entrance to his " Forum of Taurus " convincingly attests.

what could be more effective for the purpose of scaring away all evil spirits than the visible countenance of the Queen of Hell? Timomachus the painter (contemporary with the first Cæsar) made his reputation by such a subject, " præcipue tamen ars ei favisse in Gorgone visa est," are the words of Pliny, which masterpiece is supposed the original of the horrific fresco discovered at Pompeii, the finest example of the art that has reached our times. Many centuries after the fall of Paganism did this image retain its power; Münter figures ('Sinnbilder der Christen') a Gorgon's Head surrounded by the phonetic legend, +VOMΕΛΑΙΝΗΜΕΛΑΙΝΟΜΕΝΑΟCΟΦΙCΗΛΗΕC ΕΚΕΟCΛΕΟΝΒΡVΧΗCΕΙΚΕΟCΑΡΝΟCΚVΜΗCΗ,   intended   for — Υἱὸς Θεοῦ · Μελαίνη μελαινομένη, ὡς ὄφις εἴλει ἡσυχῇ, ὡς λέων βρυχήσει, καὶ ὡς ἄρνος κοιμήσει. " Black, blackened one, as a serpent thou coilest thyself quietly, thou shalt roar like a lion, thou shalt go to sleep like a lamb!" The same inscription, but so barbarously spelt as to be unintelligible, probably forms the legend upon the famous Seal of St. Servatius, preserved in Maestricht Cathedral. The seal is a large disc of green jasper, engraved on both sides, and is attached to a small slab of porphyry, traditionally passing for the Saint's portable altar. Servatius died A.D. 389, but the workmanship of his seal betokens the tenth or eleventh century for its origin. An important evidence of the veneration of the Christian Byzantines for their guardian demon is afforded by the exhumation (Spring of 1869) in the Ahmedan, Constantinople, of the Colossal Gorgonion, six feet high from chin to brow, carved in almost full relief on each side of an immense marble block, which once formed the keystone of the gateway to the Forum of Constantine. Though the execution betrays the paralysis of the Decline, yet the general effect still remains grandiose and awe-inspiring.

Having thus traced Bhavani in her progress from Archaic Greek to Byzantine times, let us observe the part she plays in the superstitions of Imperial Rome. The idea, full of novel horrors, was gladly seized by the extravagant genius of Lucan*

* Who had in all probability learnt them at some of the Mysteries, all of Asiatic origin, so popular in his times with all persons making pretensions to the title of philosophers.

to animate the exorcisms of his Thessalian sorceress Erictho
(Pharsalia, vi. 695).

" And Chaos, ever seeking to enfold
   Unnumbered worlds in thy confusion old :
And Earth's dull god, who pining still beneath
Life's lingering burthen, pinest for tardy death.
     *   *   *   *   *
Tisiphone, and Thou her sister fell,
Megaera, thus regardless of my spell,
Why haste ye not with sounding scourge to chase
The soul accursed through hell's void formless space ?
Say, must I call you by the names your right,
And drag the hell-hounds forth to th' upper light ?
Midst death I'll dog your steps at every turn,
Chase from each tomb, and drive from every urn.
And *thou*, still wont with visage not thine own,
To join the gods round the celestial throne,
Though yet thy pallor doth the truth betray,
And hint the horrors of thy gloomy   .
Thee, Hecate, in thy *true* form I'll show,
Nor let thee change the face thou wearest below.
I'll tell what feasts thy lingering steps detain
In earth's deep centre, and thy will enchain ;
Tell what the pleasures that thee so delight,
And what tie binds thee to the King of Night ;
And by what union wert thou so defiled,
Thy very mother would not claim her child,
—I'll burst thy caves, the world's most evil Lord,
And pour the sun upon thy realms abhorred,
Striking thee lifeless by the sudden day,
If still reluctant my behests to obey.
Or must I call *Him* at whose whispered *Name*
Earth trembles awestruck through her inmost frame ?
Who views the Gorgon's face without a veil,
And with her own scourge makes Erinnys quail ;
To whom the abyss, unseen by you, is given,
To which your regions are the upper heaven,
Who dares the oath that binds all gods to break,
And marks the sanction of the Stygian lake ? "

All these personifications are in a spirit quite foreign to that
of Grecian mythology, but thoroughly imbued with that of India.
Lucan's Chaos is the Hindoo Destroyer, the Negro giant, " Maha-
Pralaya," swallowing up the gods themselves in his wide-gaping
jaws. His " Rector terrae " pining for the promised annihila-
tion that is so long in coming, finds no parallel in classical

religions,* and his character remains to me utterly inexplicable. His Furies " hunting souls to make them fly," instead of being like the old awful Eumenides, the impartial avengers of guilt, are mere demons, or churchyard ghouls. But his Hecate is manifestly Bhavani herself; her " facies Erebi " being the Gorgonian aspect which the latter was when reigning in " Yama-putri," but which she puts off when presiding on earth, or in heaven ; whilst the " infernal banquets " that so enchant her are the human sacrifices regularly offered up by Bhavani's special votaries, the Thugs. In the first, or *infernal* aspect, a true " facies Erebi," she is depicted wearing a necklace of human skulls and grasping in each hand a naked victim ready to be devoured. She probably still shows us in what shape the Artemis of Pallene appeared to scare away the Ætolian plunderers. The title of her lord " pessimus mundi arbiter " is far more applicable to the Destroyer Siva than to the inoffensive Pluto of the Greeks. Unless indeed the Neronean poet may have heard something of the Demiurgus Ildabaoth, " Son of Darkness, or Erebus," existing under a different name in some ancient theogony. The Gnostics did not invent—they merely borrowed and applied.

Bhavani, in her character of " Kali," is sculptured as a terminal figure, the exact counterpart in outline of the Ephesian Diana. Even the stags, those remarkable adjuncts to the *shoulders* of the latter, are seen in a similar position spinging from Kali's *hands.* The multiplied breasts of the Ephesian statue were also given to the Alexandrian Isis, who is allowed by Creuzer and the rest to be the Hindoo goddess in her character of " Parvati." Now this remark applies only to her statue in the Serapeum, not to those belonging to the ancient Pharaonic religion ; and Macrobius's expressions show that her real character *there* was as much a matter of dispute as that of her companion, Serapis. Again, Diana as *Hecate* or Proserpine, belongs to the infernal world over which she rules with the same authority as Bhavani over Yama-Putri. The Ephesian

* Unless, perhaps, obscurely shadowed forth by Hesiod, from whom Milton drew his grand picture of Chaos, on whom wait—

" Orcus and Hades and the *dreaded Name*
Of Demogorgon."

image, made of cypress wood, had "fallen down from heaven," which only means, had come from some very remote and unknown source.

III. Monuments of the Serapis Worship.

Innumerable are the statues, bas-reliefs, and gems, many of them in the best syle of Roman art, emanating from the worship of Serapis; a thing not to be wondered at in the case of a divinity whose idea involved the two strongest principles that actuate the conduct of mankind—the love of riches and the fear of death. For the god of the subterranean world was necessarily lord also of its treasures; a truth expressed by the dedication to Serapis of an altar as "Iovi custodi et genio thesaurorum" (Winckelmann, 'Pierres Gravées de Stosch,' p. 83). And similarly the older Roman Pluto takes the title of "Jupiter Stygius;" but the comprehensiveness of the idea as expanded by the monotheistic tendency of later times is most fully manifested by the invocation (Raspe, No. 1490) ЄΙC ΖЄΥC CAPAΠΙC AΓΙΟΝ ΟΝΟΜΑ CABAW ΦWC ANATOΛΗ ΧΘWN "One Jupiter, Serapis, Holy Name, Sabaoth, the Light, the Dayspring, the Earth!'"

Talismanic gems very commonly bear the full length figure, or the bust of Serapis, with the legend ЄΙC ΘЄΟC CAPAΠΙC (often abbreviated into Є · Θ· C), "There is but one God, and he is Serapis:" ЄΙC ΖWN ΘЄΟC, "The One Living God." Sometimes the purpose of the amulet is distinctly expressed by the inscription, ΝΙΚΑΟ CAPAΠΙC ΤΟΝ ΦΘΟΝΟΝ, "Baffle the Evileye, O Serapis:" or in the curious example published by Caylus, where the god stands between Venus and Horus, and the legend ΚΑΤΑ ΧΡΗΜΑΤΙCΜΟΝ intimates that the gem had been "so" engraved in consequence of a vision or other divine intimation. Around his bust on a jasper (Praun) appears the invocation, convincing proof of his supposed supremacy, ΦΥΛΑCCЄ ΔΙΑ, "Protect Jupiter," the ancient king of heaven being now degraded to the rank of an astral genius and benignant horoscope. Invocations like the above bear the unmistakable stamp of the age when the old, liberal, mythology of the West, which had pictured Heaven as a well-ordered monarchy peopled by innumerable deities, each one having his own proper and undisputed position therein, was fast giving place to the gloomy superstitions of Syria, which made the tutelary divinity of each nation or sect the sole god of Heaven, condemning those of all other races as mere deceivers and evil spirits.

There are, however, many gems, fine both as to material and workmanship, which give us, besides Serapis, the primitive Egyptian gods exactly as they appear in the most ancient monuments, but engraved in the unmistakable style of Roman art. Most of these are to be referred to the efforts of Hadrian to resuscitate the *forms* of that old religion whose *life* had long before passed away in this equally with the grander department of sculpture. Under his zealous patronage, the religion of the Pharaohs blazed up for a moment with a brilliant but factitious lustre, a phenomenon often observed to precede the extinction of a long established system.* To this period belongs a beautiful sard of my own, which represents Serapis enthroned exactly as Macrobius describes him, whilst in front *stands* Isis, holding in one hand the sistrum, in the other a wheatsheaf, with the legend, ΗΚΥΡΙΑΕΙCΙC ΑΓΝΗ·† "Immaculate is our Lady Isis!" This address is couched in the exact words applied later to the personage who succeeded to the form, titles, symbols and ceremonies of Isis with even less variation than marked the other interchange alluded to above. The "Black Virgins" so highly venerated in certain French Cathedrals during the long night of the Middle Ages, proved when at last examined by antiquarian eyes to be basalt statues of the Egyptian goddess, which having merely changed the name, continued to receive more than pristine adoration. Her devotees carried into the new priesthood the ancient badges of their profession; "the obligation to celibacy," the tonsure, the

* Shering, in his 'Benares,' observes that the Hindoos are now building and restoring temples everywhere with greater zeal and cost than at any time since the final overthrow of Buddhism; and yet the religion itself is utterly worn out.

† In inscriptions of this period the long I is usually written EI.

bell, and the surplice—omitting unfortunately the frequent and complete ablutions enjoined by the older ritual. The holy image still moves in procession as when Juvenal laughed at it (vi. 530), "Escorted by the tonsured, surpliced, train." Even her proper title "Domina," exact translation of the Sanscrit *Isi*, survives with slight change, in the modern " Madonna " (Mater-Domina). By a singular permutation of meaning the flower borne in the hand of each, the lotus, former symbol of *perfection* (because in leaf, flower, fruit, it gave the figure of the Circle, as Jamblichus explains it), and therefore of fecundity, is now interpreted as signifying the opposite to the last—virginity itself. The tinkling *sistrum*, so well pleasing to Egyptian ears, has unluckily found a substitute in that most hideous of all noise-makers, the clangorous bell. But this latter instrument came directly from the Buddhistic ritual in which it forms as essential a part of the religion as it did in Celtic Christianity, where the Holy Bell was the actual *object* of worship to the new converts. The bell in its present form was unknown to the Greeks and Romans; its normal shape is Indian, and the first true bell-founders were the Buddhist Chinese. Again *relic-worship* became, after the third century, the chief form of Christianity throughout the world; which finds its parallel in the fact that a fragment of a bone of a Buddha (that is, holy man in whom the deity had dwelt during his life) is actually indispensable for the consecration of a *dagobah*, or temple of that religion; equally as a similar particle of saintliness is a *sine quâ non* for the setting-up of a Roman-Catholic altar.

Very curious and interesting would it be to pursue the subject, and trace how much of Egyptian, and second-hand Indian, symbolism has passed over into the possession of a church that would be beyond measure indignant at any reclamation on the part of the rightful owners. The high cap and hooked staff of the Pharaonic god become the mitre and crosier of the bishop; the very term, *Nun,* is Coptic, and with its present meaning: the erected oval symbol of productive Nature, christened into the *Vesica piscis,* becomes the proper framework for pictures of the Divinity: the *Crux ansata,* that very expressive emblem of the union of the Male and Female

Principles, whence comes all Life, and therefore placed as the symbol of Life in the hands of gods, now, by simple inversion, changes into the orb and cross, the recognised distinction of sovereignty.

But to give a last glance at Serapis and his attributes : his bust on gems is often accompanied by a figure resembling a short truncheon from the top of which spring three leaves, or spikes. Can it be some plant sacred to the god, or else some instrument of power?—certain it is that Iva, Assyrian god of Thunder, carries in his hand a *fulmen* of somewhat similar form in the Ninivitish sculptures. A dwarf column, supporting a globe, a corded bale, the letter M,* are all frequently to be seen in the same companionship. Another symbol is of such mighty import in the domains of the Lord of Souls, that its discussion may fairly claim to itself the space of the following section.

* Perhaps the Greek numeral =40, which was the number sacred to the Assyrian Hoa, god of Water. A conjecture, therefore, may be hazarded that these figures symbolise The Four Elements under the protection of the supreme Lord, Serapis.

FIG. 7.

THE *CADUCEUS*, AND ITS SYMBOLISM.

Macrobius seems to afford us some clue for solving this enigma by his remarks upon the true universality of the sun-worship under different names (Sat. i. 19). " That under the form of Mercury the *Sun* is really worshipped is evident also from the *Caduceus* which the Egyptians have fashioned in the shape of two dragons (asps), male and female joined together, and consecrated to Mercury. These serpents in the middle parts of their volume are tied together in the knot called the ' Knot of Hercules ; ' whilst their upper parts bending back-wards in a circle, by pressing their mouths together as if kissing complete the circumference of the circle ; and their tails are carried back to touch the staff of the Caduceus ; and adorn the latter with wings springing out of the same part of the staff. The meaning of the Caduceus with reference to the nativity of man, technically termed his *genesis* (or horoscope), is thus explained by the Egyptians : they teach that *four deities* preside and attend at man's birth—the Daimon (his genius), Fortune, Love, and Necessity. By the two first of these they hold that the Sun and the Moon are meant ; because the Sun, as the author of spirit, heat, and light, is the producer and guardian of human life, and therefore is esteemed the *Daimon* that is the *god* of the person born. The Moon is the *Fortune*, because she is the president over our bodies which are the sport of a variety of accidents. *Love* is signified by the kissing of the serpents ; *Necessity*, by the knot in which they are tied. The reason for adding the *wings* has been fully discussed above. For a symbol of this nature the convolution of the serpents has been selected in preference to anything else, because of the *flexuosity* of the course of both these luminaries. From this cause it comes, that the serpent is attached to the figures both of Aesculapius and of Hygiea, because these deities are explained as expressing the nature of the Sun and the Moon. For Aesculapius is the health-giving influence proceeding out of the substance of the

Sun, that benefits the souls and bodies of mortals.* Hygieia again is the influence of the nature of the Moon, by which the bodies of things animated are holpen, being strengthened by her health-giving sway. For this reason, therefore, the figure of the serpent is attached to the statues of both deities, because they bring it about that our bodies strip off, as it were, the slough of their maladies, and are restored to their pristine vigour, just as serpents renew their youth every year, by casting off the slough of old age. And the figure of the serpent is explained as an emblem of the Sun himself for the reason that the Sun is perpetually returning out of, as it were, the old age of his lowest setting, up to his full meridian height as if to the vigour of youth. Moreover, that the dragon is one of the chiefest emblems of the Sun, is manifest from the derivation of the name, it being so called from δέρκειν, 'to see.' For they teach that this serpent, by his extremely acute and never-sleeping sight, typifies the nature of the luminary; and on this account the guardianship of temples, shrines, oracles, and treasures is assigned to dragons. That Aesculapius is the same with Apollo is further proved by this fact, not merely that he is reputed the son of the latter, but because he also is invested with the privilege of divination. For Apollodorus, in his Treatise on Theology, lays down that Aesculapius presides over augury and oracles. And no wonder; seeing that the sciences of medicine and of divination are cognate sciences : for medicine predicts the changes for good or ill about to succeed in the human body. As Hippocrates hath it, the physician should be competent to predicate of his patient 'both his present, his past and future condition,' which is the same thing as divination which foreknows, as Homer says,

'The things that be, that shall be, and that were.' "

It has been already stated how, in the Mithraic worship, the image, surrounded from foot to head by the spiral convolutions of the serpent, had become the established emblem of the deity himself. The incidental remark in the above citation, that the

* Or in modern scientific phrase, *Aesculapius* is but another name for *electricity.*

N

flexuous motion of the reptile represented to the Egyptians, the annual course of the sun, affords the sufficient reason why his image should be thus encircled by so significant an attribute. Taking therefore into account the fact that the disputed symbol we are considering was by its nature primarily confined to talismans designed for medical agents, there is at once sufficient reason to suppose it connected with the worship of Aesculapius; and secondly, as it always appears in such cases in company with the Agathodæmon, the undoubted emblem of the Solar god, it may be inferred to be either a symbol or a hieroglyphical representation in little of the same type. In other words, the *figure* signifies nothing more than a serpent-entwined wand, and its *sense* only contains an allusion to the principal visible manifestation of the nature of the Sun. But this point must be left for fuller examination in its connexion with the hitherto unexplained Sigil which invariably makes its appearance on the reverse of the Chnuphis talismans, and which therefore must have been regarded as an essential element in their potency.

Fig. 8.

DEATH, AS DEPICTED IN ANCIENT ART.

The King of the Shades has formed the subject of the preceding investigation. The natural sequence of ideas requires us to consider by what visible form ancient imagination expressed the direct agency of his power, and represented to the eye the unwelcome apparition of the "Satelles Orci."

Mingling among the Cupids, whether sculptured or glyptic, and easy to be mistaken for one of the sportive group by the casual observer, comes the most popular antique embodiment of what to our notions is the most discordant of all ideas. He can only be distinguished from the God of Love by observing his pensive attitude; his action of extinguishing his torch either by striking the blazing end against the ground or by trampling it out with the foot; otherwise he leans upon it inverted, with folded wings, and arms and legs crossed in the attitude of profound repose. At other times he is divested of wings, to typify the end of all movement, and whilst he quenches his torch with one hand, he holds *behind* him with the other the large hoop, *annus* (which the Grecian Ἐνίαυτος carries *before* him), to signify that for his victim no more shall the year roll on.

To understand how so charming a type came to be appropriated to such a signification, it is necessary to cast off modern associations, and to recollect that to the ancient mind, arguing merely from the analogy of Nature, death presented itself as merely the necessary converse of birth, and consequently carried no terror in the thought—" nullique ea tristis imago," as Statius happily words it. For it implied nothing worse than the return to the state of unconsciousness, such as was before Being commenced; or, as Pliny clearly puts the case, " Unto all the state of being after the *last* day as the same as it was before the *first* day of life; neither is there any more sensation in

N 2

either body or soul after death than there was before life."
On this account the mere return, as Byron hath it—

> " To be the nothing that I was,
>   Ere born to life and living woe,"

inspired no fears beyond those springing from the natural
instinct of self-preservation. Many carried this indifference
to the opposite extreme—exemplified in the trite story of the
Thracians lamenting on the occasion of a birth, and rejoicing
on that of a death in the family. Pliny boldly declares that
the greatest favour Nature has bestowed on man is the shortness of his span of life; whilst the later Platonists, as seen
in that curious chapter of Macrobius, " On the descent of the
Soul," termed the being born into this world " spiritual
death," and dying, " spiritual birth." But after the ancient
order of ideas had been totally revolutionised—when the death
of the body came to be looked upon as the punishment of
Original Sin, and as the *infraction*, not the *fulfilment* of a
natural law—the notion necessarily assumed a more horrific
aspect; which again was exaggerated to the utmost of their
power by the new teachers, for it supplied them with the most
potent of all engines for the subjugation of the human soul—
" Æternas quoniam pœnas in morte timendum." The ancient
type, therefore, which implied nothing but peace and unbroken
repose, was therefore at once discarded, as totally inconsistent
with the altered view of the reality. Add to this the fact that
everything in the shape of Cupid had been forcibly enrolled
amongst the Cherubim and Seraphim, and had thereby received
a character yet more foreign to that of the newly-created King
of Terrors.

Hence the Christians were driven to seek in the ancient
iconology for a more fitting representation of the offspring and
avenger of transgression—something that should be equally
ghastly and terror-inspiring—and such a representative they
found made to their hand in the former way of picturing a
Larva, or bad man's ghost. This had always been depicted as
a *skeleton*, and such a figure was recommended by old asso-
ciation to their minds in the times when (as Böttiger phrases
it) " the Christians creeping forth out of their catacombs

substituted for the Genius with inverted torch, the skulls and mouldering bones of their own martyrs." And that the *larva* was popularly imagined in a skeleton form, appears, amongst the rest, from Ovid's line in his 'Ibis'—

"Insequar atque oculos *ossea* larva tuos."
"Where'er thou turn'st my injured shade shall rise,
 And flit, a fleshless ghost before thine eyes."

Seneca also laughs at the vulgar notion of "larva-forms, frames of bare bones hanging together;" and Trimalchio, at his famous dinner, in order to promote conviviality, throws down upon the table a silver larva, so ingeniously made as to bound about on the board with every limb quivering, whilst the host hiccups out the admonition—

"Heu, Heu, nos miseros, quam totus homuncio nil est,
 Sic erimus cuncti, postquam nos auferet Orcus
 Ergo vivamus dum licet esse bene."

Such a larva sometimes makes his appearance on the gem, introduced there for the same purpose—to remind his wearer of the shortness of life, and the wisdom of making the best use of the portion allotted to him—speaking, mutely, the words of Virgil's 'Copa Syrisca'—

"Pone merum et talos, pereat qui crastina curat!
 Mors aurem vellens; Vivite, ait, venio."

Thus upon one gem we behold him holding forth in his bony hand the *lecythus* (long, pointed vase of oil), that regularly accompanied every Greek interment, whilst he leans with his elbow against a huge *amphora* of wine, as though recommending the enjoyment of its contents whilst yet in one's power.* Another, a more fanciful composition, depicts Cupid casting the light of his torch into the depths of an immense Corinthian *crater* out of which a skeleton is throwing himself headlong, as though scared away by the hateful glare—a design whose abstruse meaning may perhaps be interpreted by the foregoing

* Exactly the same lesson is taught by a drinking-cup in the Orléans Museum, the decoration of which is a dance of skeletons. (Mém. Soc. Antiq. de France, vol. xxxi.)

remarks ('Impronte Gemmarie,' ii. 10, 11).* A skeleton, likewise, was often painted on the wall of tombs; for example, in that
pathetic scene at Pompeii, where a mother is represented laying
a mortuary fillet over the bones of her child. In all these
cases the form is merely intended to symbolise the *condition* of
death by placing before the eye the body as deserted by life,
reduced to the state most expressive of mortality and decay,
and which cannot be mistaken for one of sleep. But it is easy
to perceive how ready was the transition from the hieroglyph
of mortality regarded as a *state* (especially when to the popular
mind the figure also represented a restless and malignant
spiritual being) to the adoption of the same inauspicious shape
for the embodiment of the idea of the actual principle of
destruction.

But to return to antique imagery of the same sense. The
idea of death is ingeniously and curiously expressed in a fresco
decorating the lately discovered vault of Vincentius and Vibia,
in the Catacombs of Prætextatus, Rome. In the scene labelled
"abreptio Vibie et Discensio," the messenger of Fate, "Mer-
curius," appears placing one foot and leading the way into a
huge *urn* laid sideways on the ground. The allusion to *Orcus*
in the name of such a vessel, *orca*, is sufficiently obvious, and
in fact both may spring from the same root, ἕρκος, *inclosure*,
prison. But the most common type, perpetually repeated on
sarcophagi and tablets, is the *Horse*, significant of departure,
looking in through the window upon a party carousing—
life's festive scene. Yet more forcibly is the same notion
carried out in an Etruscan sculpture (figured in the Revue
Archéologique, 1844), where the angel of death, *Charun*, armed
as usual with his ponderous mall, actually leads this horse
upon which sits the deceased with head muffled up, "capite
obnupto"—the established form in sentencing a criminal to
execution. The same reason, probably, made the horse's head

* Such a larva also points the
moral of the scene embossed upon a
lamp, published by De Witte (Mem.
Soc. Antiq de France, 1871), where
a philosopher seated, and grasping a
scroll, is apostrophising a skeleton
standing before him; at his feet lies
an infant in swaddling-clothes. These
adjuncts declare the subject of the
philosopher's meditations—the des-
tiny of Man from birth to death.

so popular a subject for signet-gems; it served there for a *memento-mori*, like the death's heads so much in vogue amongst the jewels of the Cinque-cento time, although the antique symbol carried with it a widely different admonition. The same notion may possibly lie at the bottom of that immemorial custom in South Wales of the mummers carrying the skull of a horse in their Christmas merry-makings.

Cognate to this is that most ancient representation of the conveyance of the departed soul to the realms of bliss—imagined as some happy island in the far West—upon a fantastic hippocampus, in figure like a winged sea-serpent, and who later became the Roman Capricornus, "Ruler of the Hesperian Wave:"—

> "Thou, for thy rule, O Capricorn! hast won
> All that extends beneath the setting sun,"

as Manilius defines the authority of that amphibious sign. But the original conception is often engraved upon Phœnician scarabic; and no doubt can remain as to its intention, since Caylus has published an Etruscan vase (i. pl. 32) where this same monster is painted joyously careering over the sea, whilst on its other side stands the mourner, *præfica*, chaunting the funeral hymn over the corpse laid out upon its bier of bronze.

To continue within the earliest portion of the subject, it must be observed that in the most ancient monument of Greek sculpture wheieof any account remains—the Coffer of Cypselus (executed earlier than 600 B.C.)—*Night* was represented carrying in her arms two children, alike in all respects save colour; the one white, the other black, having their *legs crossed*:* their names being inscribed over them—*Sleep* and *Death*—for their mother was hastening to the aid of the expiring Memnon. Thus it is manifest that from the very dawn of pictorial art the *crossed legs* were the accepted emblem of the most profound repose; whilst the sluggard's wish for " a little more folding of

---

* διεστραμμένους τοὺς πόδας. The very obvious meaning of these words critics have contrived to misunderstand, and to render as "distorted." Nor is this all; entirely upon the authority of this blunder, Propertius' "somnia *vana*" have been turned into "somnia *vara*," and ever since the whole tribe of Dreams are believed to walk *bandy-legged*.

the hands in slumber" bears the same testimony to the import of
the *crossed arms* of the Roman Genius who leans on his inverted
torch.   In that master-piece of Roman chasing, the Pompeian
discus, "The Death of Cleopatra," the object of the design is
indicated with equal truth and pathos by the placing of the
beauteous infant genius at the knee of the dying queen, on
which he rests his elbow to form a support for his head as
though dropping off into a gentle slumber.   The traditional
attitude* retained its significancy well understood far down
into the Middle Ages : witness so many cross-legged effigies
of warriors resting from their toils—who for that sole reason
popularly pass for crusaders.

But in the whole long catalogue of emblems, not one
expressed the *abstract* idea so definitely as that most frequently
employed in such sense—the Gorgon's Head.   Accepting the
explanation already offered (p. 167), that at its origin this
terrific visage was designed for the "vera effigies" of the Queen
of the dead, it was the most speaking emblem of her office that
could possibly be chosen.   In the Heroic ages it was universally
painted, or embossed upon the warrior's shield ; and with the
progress of art, cut in cameo, became the regular decoration of
the imperial breastplate ; † in which post it served, as Lucian
remarks ('Philopatris'), "both to terrify enemies and to avert
all danger from the wearer," conveying to all beholders the
menace of death exactly as now by an undesigned coincidence
does the death's head and cross-bones painted upon the pirate's
flag.   The Byzantines, in the true spirit of their gloomy superstition, discarded the Præ-Italian type for whose beauty they
had lost all feeling, and reverted to the image invented by the
horror-loving genius of Pelasgic barbarism.   They saw in it
the most faithful representation of their Μοῖρα, the destroying
demon or *ghoul*, still believed by the Greek peasant to haunt

---

* The child's skeleton in the
Pompeian painting above quoted,
similarly folds his feet.

† Accipe belligeræ crudum thoraca
　　Minervæ,
　Ipsa Meduseæ quam timet ira
　　comæ.

Dum vacat hæc, Cæsar, poterit
　lorica vocari,
Pectore cum sacro sederit, Ægis
　erit.
　　　　　　　　· Mart.' vii. 1.

ruins and desolate places. That the figure was received in such a sense into Byzantine symbolism, the examples of amulets already quoted convincingly declare. From Byzantine the Gorgon passed into Gothic art, which ever revelling in grotesque horror, its inspiring genius being the *skeleton* which intrudes his ghastliness into every mode of ornamentation, even of a mirror-frame (Lucrezia Borgia's for example) contrived to render the image yet more terrible by converting the face into a fleshless skull, and substituting for the hawk's wings lent by Hermes, which previously impelled its flight, the skinny pinions of her own congenial and much-loved fowl, the sepulchre-haunting *bat*.

But of all these emblems, not one is so full of poetry and truth as the device of the *Winged Foot* crushing the Butterfly, Life. The Foot, chosen probably for the same reason as the Horse, as conveying most speakingly the notion of *departure*, was equally accepted as the emblem of death. Horace's simile must occur to every reader :—

> " Pallida Mors æquo pulsat *pede* pauperum tabernas
> Regumque turres."

On this account the Foot became the peculiar attribute of the infernal deities; and the figure of one carved in stone was often dedicated in the temple of Serapis *—apparently as an *ex voto* commemorating the donor's escape from the very threshold of his dark domain. Singularly related to this custom is what Moor notices of the pairs of feet carved in stone commonly seen in the vicinity of Hindoo temples, traditionally said to be memorials of *suttees*, marking the spot whence the devoted widow stepped from earth upon the funeral pile, that is into the Gate of Heaven.

It has long been a question how the Grecian *Hades* (" The Invisible One ") and the Roman *Pluto* were depicted in a bodily form as they were originally conceived—for their *Egyptian* equivalent, Serapis, figures much more frequently in

---

* A colossal example of the finest workmanship was exhumed at Alexandria a few years ago. It may have been contemporary with the coin of Commodus from that mint, which has for reverse a head of Serapis placed upon a foot for pedestal, with the date of his seventh year.

monuments of Imperial date than either of his brethren, Jove or Neptune. In the latter style he is regularly sculptured as *Plutus*, "Lord of Riches," seated on a throne, holding a cornucopia, and extending with his right hand a cluster of earth's choicest gifts. But under what form the primitive Greeks had imagined their Aïdoneus, God of the Shades, before Serapis was introduced into their mythology, is a question that has never been satisfactorily answered. We should have found him on the scarabeus of the Etruscans and early Italiotes, had not a long-enduring respect for things divine (expressly enjoined by Pythagoras) prevented their placing in their signets, used for everyday purposes, the actual figures of the gods, whose absence they supplied by their well-known attributes. For this reason a popular Etruscan seal-device is Cerberus, represented sometimes as a man with three heads of a dog, but more commonly in the shape so familiar to us from later arts. But the Egyptians had contrived to make their Guardian of the Shades much more formidable in aspect by equipping him with the heads of a lion, crocodile, and hippopotamus. We are also certified in what shape the Etruscans imaged their god of the lower world, *Mantus*; for he is painted with serpent legs, like Typhon, wielding a huge butcher's cleaver, and attended by Cerberus, enthroned upon the court placed below the niche of interment, *loculus*, in the Campana tomb, Cervetri.

The "Helmet of Hades" is named by Homer (v. 845), which Pallas puts on in order to render herself invisible to Ares; which *helmet* the scholiast explains by "cloud and invisibility"—whence it seems but natural to infer that, as this deity was rendered *invisible* by his very attribute, no attempt would be made to depict his personal appearance. A figure of a god in long flowing robes, and wielding a trident wanting one of its prongs, sometimes painted on the Nolan vases, has been taken for an Aïdoneus, but on no sufficient grounds, there being better reason to consider him a Poseidon in the archaic style. The epithet "Renowned for horses" is given to the same god elsewhere by Homer (v. 445), allusive doubtless to the *swiftness* of the Destroyer : and in the same title may, perchance, lie the motive which made the Greeks adopt the *horse*, as above noticed, for the commonest symbol of his power. If we could meet with any genuine antique and *early* representation of the Rape of Proserpine it would at once decide the question by portraying the grim Ravisher himself; but the inauspicious nature of the subject (so conspicuously set forth in Suetonius' anecdote of the ring with the story presented by Sporus to Nero for a New Year's gift) has completely excluded it from the artist's repertory, so far as anything now remaining informs us. Stosch's Collection, amongst its immense varity of mythological designs, contains nothing of the sort, whilst Raspe gives for its representative only a single antique paste (and that, too, of very dubious attribution) where a god with quiver on shoulder is carrying off a Nymph in a car drawn by two swans—attributes properly bespeaking an Apollo; and if really given here to Pluto, proving the work to belong to those latter times of Paganism when Hades, Serapis, Phœbus, were equally interpreted as mere titles of the Solar god.

As for the Roman Pluto, or, to give him his native name, *Dis* (*ditis*, from the same root as *death*), there was the best of reasons for excluding him from the province of art which admitted nought that was hideous or of evil augury. For there can be no doubt, that, to the popular imagination, he still continued the *Charun,** whom we still behold lording it over the sepulchres of their Etruscan teachers in the arts, a giant of horrid aspect with pointed ears, and tusky grinning jaws, winged buskins on legs, extending with one hand a hissing serpent, with the other wielding a monstrous mall. It was probably the traditional influence of the idea that caused the same instrument, *mazza*, to be retained at Rome for the execution of peculiarly atrocious criminals down to the recent introduction of the guillotine.

That Pluto was really so personified in the shows of the Amphitheatre, as late as the third century, may be gathered from the remark of Tertullian (Apol. xxv.), that, "amongst the other scenic cruelties of the afternoon, the spectators laughed at the sight of Mercury raising the dead with his *red-hot* wand [applied doubtless to the feet of the slaughtered gladiators to

* As Etruria was the only school of art for Rome until very late times, she supplied the *figures* equally with the *names* of all the Roman deities.

ascertain if life still lingered within them]; whilst the 'Brother of Jupiter,' armed with his *mall*, escorted the dead bodies of the combatant " [for the purpose clearly of giving them the *coup de grâce*]. The primitive Etruscan image passed down into the belief of their mediæval descendants, for Dante brings on the stage :—

" Charon, demonio con occhi di bragia."
" *Charon, a devil with live-coals for eyes.*"

It is time now to dismiss the Lord of the Shades, and to consider by what *Emblem* ancient art sought to express the *Shade* itself, the disembodied spirit. The Greeks of early times appropriately painted it in the shape of a *bird* with a human head, as on that beautiful vase, "The Death of Procris" (British Museum), where such a fowl is conspicuously seen winging its flight from the mouth of the wounded Nymph. The celebrated Orléans (now Russian) scarabeus, engraved with the "Death of Achilles," has its back carved into the same creature, tearing her breast in an agony of despair. This expressive type was not, however, the birth of Grecian genius, but adopted, without alteration, from the most ancient symbolism of Egypt. In the "Judgment of the body and soul," regularly painted on the mummy-cases, the former, depicted as a mummy, stands before Osiris, "Lord of the West," to answer for its *actions;* whilst the soul, in shape of a hawk, with human head and wings uplifted, is brought before the same god under another form, to give an account of its *thoughts.* And the same soul, purified, and admitted amongst the gods, appears as before, but tranquilly standing with a golden disk, "a crown of glory," set upon her head : figures of the last kind in bronze frequently occurring amongst Egyptian remains, complimentary mementoes of deceased friends. Again, this same bird is often found painted on the mummy-case right over the *heart* (named in Coptic, "the abode of the soul"), a plain proof of what it signifies there; although Father Kircher, with his wonted extravagance, chose to explain it as figuring the *iynx*, the bird so renowned in the magical operations of the Greeks. Again, the same notion is expressed by the simple figure of a bird flying away, as often is done in Etruscan works, where the subject represented is the

death of a hero. Latest of all, this somewhat grotesque
Egyptian conception was modified by Grecian culture into the
graceful girl with butterfly wings—the well-known Psyche—
and such a form is seen seated upon the summit of Achilles'
tomb, before which the sacrifice of Polyxena is about to be
offered. This ancient human-headed Bird, by a natural transition of ideas, came ultimately to be applied to express a
widely different meaning. Instead of the *dead*, it was made to
stand for the *destroyer*; and the Syrens are always painted in
this shape whenever their interview with Ulysses becomes the
theme of ancient art, or when they engage in their unlucky
contest with the Muses. But here, for the sake of more grace,
in the conformation of the monster, the whole of the female
bust is adapted to the body of the fowl. Despite their beauty
and melodiousness, the Syrens were considered as the most
malignant and destructive of beings, for which reason the
Harpies likewise were depicted in precisely the same figure.
Although identical at first, the more refining art of Roman
times introduced a distinction between them by giving to the
Syrens the complete *bust*, to the Harpies the *head* only of the
woman. Inasmuch as the name signifies "Snatcher-away," the
Harpy was understood to embody the abstract idea of death,
which acceptation explains why she is often represented armed
with a sword, or carrying on her shoulder the funeral *lecythus*,
and torch. For the same reason the Harpy holds a conspicuous
place in the decorations of many ancient tombs, unlesss, indeed,
the emblem may have been used there in its Egyptian sense.

In what shape Death was personified by Euripides, in his
Alcestis, cannot be made out from the insufficiency of data
afforded by the lines relating to his appearance on the stage.
It is, however, plain that the poet brought forward Θάνατος in
a bodily form, perhaps considering him the same with Aïdoneus,
for he styles him "King of the Dead;" and Macrobius, speaking
of the same event, uses for his name the Roman equivalent,
"Orcus." All that can be gathered from the incidental allu-
sions of the other *dramatis personæ* to this apparition, is that he
was robed in *black*, and carried a *sword*, wherewith to sever a
lock from the head of his destined victim, and so devote it to

the subterranean gods. It is, however, possible that Euripides brought on this Θάνατος in that harpy shape which sometimes is found in antique art where the bust is that of a grim aged man, in place of the smiling female's, and who, as badge of office, carries a naked *sword*. In such a form the Destroyer must have flitted before the eyes of Statius, when about to make prey of the young and beautiful Glaucius :—

> "Subitas inimica levavit
> Parca manus; quo diva feros gravis exuis *ungues?*"

This last word can apply to nothing but the Harpy, of whom *claws* were the distinctive attribute :—

> "*Unguibus* ire parat nummos raptura Celæno." *

Nevertheless, a representation like this had in it nothing grotesque or offensive to the Athenian eye. Far different was the Pelasgic Κῆρ, likewise *robed in black* (according to Homer's normal epithet for her), in the form which the archaic sculptor had given her upon the Coffer of Cypselus, "having tusks as fierce as those of any wild beast." Such a conception was eagerly embraced by the gloomy genius of the Etruscans, ever delighting in the monstrous and the horrible. She therefore figures on their signets in a form to be described in the very words of Pausanias, having a huge Gorgonian head, grinning jaws, arms wreathed with serpents, impelled by quadruple wings, like an Assyrian deity, and her action that of furious haste. So, doubtless, appeared the Furies, brought on the stage by Æschylus, when the horror of their strange aspect struck the Athenian audience with such deadly fright. For his purpose he must have revived a very ancient and *forgotten* type of the idea, for the paintings on the vases of his epoch exhibit the Eumenides, who persecute Orestes, under a no more terrific form than as shadowy old women brandishing serpents and torches, as they chase their victim from shrine to shrine.

---

* The same picture must have been in Horace's mind when he uses the figure .   .   .   .
> "Mors atris circumvolat alis."

TOMB-TREASURES.

Serapis, in his double character of God of Death and God of Riches, has been the subject of preceding chapters; the present one shall be devoted to the consideration of the most striking method by which human superstition sought to turn to account the two ideas. To propitiate the *Manes* by placing his most valuable or beloved effects in the sepulchre of the defunct, dates probably from the very institution of interment; but the account now to be cited is the most interesting of any on record, owing to the circumstances of the time, person, and place. It is literally translated from the description of an eye witness, the earliest of Italian antiquaries, M. L. Fauno, given in his 'Antichita de Roma,' p. 154, published 1553.

"In February, 1544, in the Chapel of the King of France, which is now being built in St. Peter's, after the plan of Julius II., the workmen, in excavating, came upon a marble coffin, which, from the things found therein, was clearly known to be the tomb of Maria, wife of the Emperor Honorius. Of the body, indeed, there was nothing left, except the teeth, the hair, and the two leg-bones. From the robes which were interwoven with gold, and from the head-tire, which was cloth of silk and gold, there was extracted by smelting more than *forty* pounds weight of the purest gold." [Suecius says *thirty-six*, but makes the total of all the gold found to amount to the above weight when they were melted down by order of Paul III., to be applied to the building fund of the Cathedral.]

" Within the coffin lay a silver box, one and a half foot long by eight inches deep, with many articles inside, the which we shall proceed particularly to describe. There were vases and different things in rock crystal, thirty in all, big and little; amongst which were two cups, as it were, not very large, the one round, the other oval shaped, with most beautiful figures in intaglio of middling depth (*mezzo-cavo*), and a *snail-shell* (nautilus), likewise in crystal, fitted up for a lamp in fine gold, with which in the first place the mouth of the shell is overlaid, there being only left a hole for pouring in the oil; by the side of which hole is fixed a *fly* of gold upon a pivot, turning backwards and forwards, for the purpose of closing the orifice. In the same way is also made a nozzle with beak (*pippio*) for holding the wick, drawn out long and sharpened with the greatest elegance, and so fastened to the crystal that it appears all one piece naturally. The cover also is equally well made. The shape of the shell is that of a great sea-shell, encompassed all round with its points, which in this vessel are polished and very smooth, so excellently wrought is the crystal. There were also vases and various articles in agate, with certain little animals, eight in all, and amongst them two very beautiful vases, one like the glass *ampullae*, made big and squat for holding oil and such like liquids, so worked, so beautiful, and thin that it is a wonder to behold. The other is in the shape of those ladles with long handles used at Rome for baling water out of cisterns, and is supposed to be a vessel used by the ancients in their sacrifices [a *ligula* for the purpose of ladling the wine out of the great standing *crater*]. Next came four little vessels in gold of different kinds, and another little vessel of gold with a cover set round with jewels. A little gold heart that had been a pendant with jewels set in it; a buckle of gold with six gems of different kinds set in it; also twenty-four other buckles of gold of various patterns with little gems set in them; furthermore, forty-eight rings and *hoops** of gold of different shapes, one of them in red bone, and various gems. A mouse in "chelidonia," a reddish quartz, is also specified by Suecius [which must be the next item], also three little animals in *red bone*; also two ear-drops in emerald or plasma with two jacinths; four small crosses with red and green stones; a pendant in the form of a bunch of grapes, made of purple stones; eight other little gold pendants of different sorts with gems set in them. The remains of a string of *crepundia*, the usual decoration of little children. [Maria had died at the age of *four*, being thus early betrothed to Honorius by his father the all-powerful Stilicho]. Three little gold crosses set with emeralds; a piece of a small fine necklace with certain green

---

* *Verghe:* "verga," like the French verge, signifies a plain gold wire forming a ring having no head.

stones strung upon it. Another little gold necklace with twenty-four beads of plasma. Another necklace with twelve heads of sapphire cut almond shape. Another little necklace of gold wire folded up (*raccolto*), but broken into four pieces. Two small buttons in gold; fourteen little gold-wire rings like those of a coat of mail; three more crosses with some emeralds, and a round gold plate like an Agnus Dei,* with these words upon it, STILICHO VIVAT. Two bracelets (*maniche*) of gold, set with certain red and green stones. Two large pins or *stiletti* for the hair, one in gold nearly a palm (nine inches) long inscribed with these words, DOMINVS HONORIVS DOMINA MARIA : the other in silver without inscription. There were likewise many fragments of enamels and other stones. Also silver nails [their heads] partly flat, partly in relief, which had fastened down a cover of silver upon a little coffer. Also a small plate of gold with these words written or rather *scratched* in Greek, MICHAEL· GABRIEL· RAPHAEL· VRIEL·" [Laurentius Surius makes out *forty* gold rings set with precious stones, besides an emerald set in gold, engraved with a head supposed to be that of Honorius, which was valued at five hundred gold ducats]. We have particularly described all the above-named objects because Claudian, a poet of those times, declares that to the Empress Maria were sent similar rare presents from her betrothed; which perhaps may have formed the greatest part of these things. The words of the poet are—

> " Jam munera nuptæ
> Præparat, et pulchros Mariæ sed luce minores
> Elicit ornatus : quidquid venerabilis olim
> Livia, divorumque nurus gessere superbæ." (x. 10–13.)

This account enables us to form some notion of the treasures deposited to a greater or less degree in all the tombs of important personages, but more especially in those sumptuous structures raised to the memory of the dead throughout Asia Minor. The same fact sufficiently accounts for the furious onslaught made upon the tombs all over the Roman world, so soon as the change of religion had extinguished the old veneration for the *Manes* and the things consecrated to them—a profanation, and a

---

* A disk of stamped wax about three inches in diameter.

destruction of works of art, which Gregorius Theologus, inspired by a taste and good feeling very surprising in a Byzantine saint, has attacked in one hundred and eighty-two very interesting and often poetical epigrams.

The same custom was kept up (although we can hardly suppose with any lingering belief in its ancient efficiency) by the Merovingian and Carlovingian successors to the wealth of the Western Empire. The learned Canon Chiflet has left in his interesting book, 'Anastasis Childerici Regis,' a complete history of tomb-treasures, serving to illustrate his account of that of Childeric the Frank, accidentally found in the precincts of Tournay Cathedral, May 1654. The deposit, as far it could be recovered from the first finders, consisted of the arms of the king, the trappings of his horse (buried with him), all of gold encrusted with garnets, his gold tablets and writing-stylus, abundance of golden-bees originally stretched over his mantle (which gave that curious idea to Napoleon I.), a bull's head for a pendant (the primitive Frankish badge of sovereignty), and lastly, a *viaticum* in the shape of one hundred Byzantine *solidi* of contemporary emperors, and as many denarii of several and much earlier Cæsars. The canon, by zealous perquisitions, succeeded in recovering all these articles, including the most important of all, the royal signet ring of massy gold, engraved with the image and superscription of Childeric, for his patron the Archduke Leopold, then governor of the Low Countries. At some subsequent period the most important of these relics passed into the collection of the Bibliothèque Impériale, where they continued in all due honour until the disastrous robbery of 1808, when it is supposed, with too much probability, that they were melted down along with the rest of the booty !

FIG. 9.

GNOSTIC CONNECTION WITH SUPERSTITIOUS PRACTICES.

I. THE EVIL EYE.

Serapis we have seen, in one of his representations lately noticed, specially invoked to defend his votary against the *Evil Eye* under its abstract title of φθόνος. A glance therefore at this most ancient superstition (which still flourishes in full vigour in the same countries that gave it birth) will form a fitting prelude to the coming section, which takes for subject talismans and amulets of every class.

The belief in the power for mischief of the eye of an envious or malignant person (to counteract which was the principal object of so many of the amulets that have come down to us) was universal amongst all ancient nations. It is needless to bring forward classic writers to support this statement; such as Apollonius Rhodius, where he skilfully avails himself of the notion, and makes Medea by her basilisk glance alone work the death of Talas, the Brazen Man, guardian of the Cretan shores; for even St. Paul (Rom. i. 29) sets down this action of the soul working through the eye in the list of sins of the deepest dye. But the actual *manner* of operation upon the sufferer I have nowhere found explained except in the following passage from Heliodorus ('Æthiopica,' iii. 8), and which therefore deserves to be inserted at length in this prelude to the subject. "Tell me, my good Calasiris, what is the malady that has attacked your daughter?" "You ought not to be surprised," I replied, "if at the time when she was heading the procession in the sight of so vast an assemblage of people, she had drawn upon herself some *envious eye*." Whereupon, smiling ironically, "Do you then," asked he, "like the vulgar in general, believe in the reality of such fascination?" "As much as I do in any other fact," I replied, "and the thing is this: the air which surrounds us passing through the eyes, as it were through a strainer, and also through the mouth, the teeth and the other passages, into the inward parts, whilst its external properties make their way in together with it—whatever be its quality as it flows in, of the same nature is the effect it disseminates in the recipient, so that when any one looks upon beauty with envy, he fills the circumambient air with a malignant property, and diffuses upon his neighbour the breath issuing from himself, all impregnated with bitterness, and *this*, being as it is of a most subtile nature, penetrates through into the very bone and marrow. Hence envy has frequently turned itself into a regular disease, and has received the distinctive appellation of *fascination* (βασκανία). Consider also, my Charicles, how many people have been infected with ophthalmia, how many with other pestilential diseases, not from any contact with those so affected, or from sharing the same bed or same table, but merely from breathing the same air. Let also (and above all the rest), the origin of love be a support to my argument, for *that* owes its first origin to the sight which shoots like arrows the passion into the soul. And for this there is very good reason, for of all the senses and passages of the body, the sight is the most easily excited, and the most inflammable, and consequently the most susceptible with regard to external emanation, in consequence of its own natural fiery essence, attracting to itself the visits of love. And if you wish for a proof drawn from Natural History, recorded likewise in the Sacred Books, the bird, the yellow-hammer, cures the jaundice, and if a person so affected shall but look at that bird, the latter at once tries to escape and shuts its eyes ; not as some think, because it begrudges the benefit to the sick man, but because, if looked upon by men, it is forced by its nature to attract his disease into its own body, like an exhala-tion, and therefore shuns the glance as much as a blow. And amongst serpents, the basilisk, doth not he, as you may have heard, kill and blast whatever comes in his way by means of his eyes and his breath alone ? And if some give the stroke of the Evil Eye even to those they love and are well disposed towards, you must not be surprised, for people of an envious disposition act not as they *wish*, but as their Nature *compels* them to do."

II. On a Ceraunia of Jade Converted into a Gnostic Talisman.

Few relics of antiquity combine in one so many and so widely differing points of interest, with respect to the material, the strangely dissimilar uses to which the same object has been applied in two opposite phases of the history of Man, and, above all, the curious superstitions engendered by its peculiar form, as does the stone brought under the notice of the Archæological Institute by General Lefroy, now in the Woolwich Repository. The kindness of that gentleman having afforded me full opportunity for the careful examination of this interesting monument, I proceed to embody, in as succinct a form as their multifarious nature will permit, the observations suggested to me by that examination.

The subject, therefore, of this section is a small stone celt of the common pattern, but of very uncommon material (in the *antique* class), being made, not of flint, but of dark-green jade or nephrite, 2 in. by 1½ in. in length and greatest width; and brought, there is reason to believe, from Egypt many years ago, by Colonel Milner, aide-de-camp to Lord J. Bathurst during the English occupation of Sicily in 1812. Each of its two faces is occupied by a Gnostic formula, engraved with much neatness, considering the excessive hardness of the material, in the somewhat debased Greek character that was current at Alexandria during the third and fourth centuries of our era.

The most important of these two formulæ has been ingeniously forced to take the outline of a wreath composed of broad leaves, in number *fourteen* (or the sacred *seven* duplicated), and doubtless intended for those of the "Five Trees" that figure so conspicuously in Gnostic symbolism; the ends being tied together with four broad ribbons. This is a design of which no other example has ever come to my knowledge amongst the innumerable and wondrously varied devices excogitated by the prolific fancy of this religion of mysteries. Upon the four ties are engraved in very minute letters different combinations of the seven Greek vowels, whilst each of the leaves is emblazoned with some "Holy Name," of which many can be easily recognised as constantly recurring in charms of this class; others are disguised by a novel orthography; whilst a few, from the uncertain forms of the lettering, defy all attempts at interpretation.

To the first series belong ABPACA, "Abraxas," properly an epithet of the sun, but designating here the Supreme Deity; IAШOYIE, "Iao, Jehovah;" ABΛANA, "Thou art our Father!" ΓAMBPIHΛ, a curious mode of spelling "Gabriel," that testifies to the difficulty ever felt by the Greeks of expressing the sound of our B; AKTNONBШ, which contains the Coptic form of Anubis; ΔAMNAMENEYC, the sun's name in the famous "Ephesian Spell;" and, most interesting of all, ΠCANTAPEOC, who can be no other than the IΨANTA of the *Pistis-Sophia*— one of the great Tριδυνάμεις, a Power from whom is enthroned in the planet *Mars.* To the uncertain belong COYMA, probably for COYMAPTA, a name occurring elsewhere, and perhaps cognate to the Hindoo *Sumitri*, XШNONIXAP which may be intended for XAP-XNOYMIC, a common epithet of the Agathodæmon Serpent; AEIШEHAANHC; NEIXAPOΠΛHC; the two last, spells unexplained but very uncommon; MONAPXOC; whilst AXAPCIC and the rest appear here for the first time, if correctly so read.

The other face is covered with an inscription, cut in much larger letters, and in *eight* lines. This number was certainly not the result of chance, but of deep design, for it was mystic in the highest degree, representing—so taught the profoundest doctor of the Gnosis, Marcus—the divine Ogdoad, which was the daughter of the Pythagorean Tetrad, the mother of all creation.* The lines 2, 4, 5, consist of Greek letters used as *numerals*, intermixed with *siglæ*, which, from their constant occurrence upon monuments of a like nature, are supposed, with good reason, to be symbols of the planets. The numerals, on their part, probably denote various deities, for the Alexandrian Gnosis was the true daughter of Magiism; and in the old theology of Chaldea every god and astral genius had a *number* of his own, and which often stands instead of his proper

* St. Hippolytus, Refut. Om. Hæres. vi. 50.

name in dedicatory inscriptions.* Thus, the number of Hoa (Neptune), was 40; of Ana (Pluto), 60; of Bel (Jupiter), 50; of the Sun, 20; of the moon, 30; of the Air, 10; of Nergal (Mars), 12; &c.

A fragment of the *Pistis-Sophia*† supplied the "spiritual man" with a key to the right interpretation of similar steno- graphy in his own creed. "These be the *Names* which I will give unto thee, even from the Infinite One downwards. Write the same with a sign (cypher), so that the sons of God may manifest (understand?) them out of this place. This is the name of the Immortal One, $\overline{AAA}$ $\overline{\omega\omega\omega}$.‡ And this is the name of the Voice whereby the Perfect Man is moved, $\overline{III}$. These likewise be the interpretations of the names of the Mysteries. The first is AAA, and the interpretation thereof is ΦΦΦ. The second, which is MMM, or which is ωωω, the interpretation thereof is AAA. The third is ΨΨΨ, the inter- pretation thereof is OOO. The forth is ΦΦΦ, the interpretation thereof is NNN. The fifth ΔΔΔ, the interpretation thereof is AAA, the which is above the throne of AAA. This is the in- terpretation of the second AAAA, namely, AAAAAAAA; the same is the interpretation of the whole Name."

Lines 7, 8, are made up of vowels, variously combined, and shrouding from profane eyes the *Ineffable Name* $\overline{IA\Omega}$ which, as we are informed by many authorities (the most ancient and trustworthy being Diodorus Siculus),§ was the name of the God of the Jews; meaning thereby their mode of writing "Jehovah" in Greek characters.

Line 3 consists of the seven vowels placed in their natural order. This was the most potent of all the spells in the Gnostic repertory; and its importance may justify the ex- tensiveness of the following extract from the grand text-book of this theosophy, which sets forth its hidden sense and wondrous efficacy. The primary idea, however, was far from abstruse, if we accept the statement of the writer "On Interpre-

---

* On this curious subject, see Rawlinson's 'Ancient Monarchies,' iii. p. 466.

† Cap. 125.

‡ That is, 1000 and 800 tripled. The next numbers are 10,000 tripled, and so on.

§ 'Bibliotheca Historica,' i. 94.

tations," that the Egyptians expressed the name of the Supreme
God by the seven vowels thus arranged—ΙΕΗΩΟΥΑ.* But
this single mystery was soon refined upon, and made the basis
of other and infinitely deeper mysteries. In an inscription
found at Miletus (published by Montfaucon), the Holy ΙΕΟΥ-
ΑΗΩΑΕΙΟΥΩ is besought "to protect the city of Miletus
and all the inhabitants of the same; a plain proof that this
interminable combination only expressed the name of some *one*
divine being. Again, the *Pistis-Sophia* perpetually brings in
ΙΕΟΥ invariably accompanied with the epithet of "the Primal
Man," *i.e.*, He after whose image or *type* man was first created.
But in the fulness of time the semi-Pythagorean, Marcus, had
it revealed unto him that the seven heavens in their revelation
sounded each one vowel which, all combined together, formed a
single doxology, "the sound whereof being carried down to
earth becomes the creator and parent of all things that be on
earth."†

The Greek language has but one word for *vowel* and *voice*;
when therefore, "the seven thunders uttered their voices," the
seven vowels, it is meant, echoed through the vault of heaven,
and composed that mystic utterance which the sainted seer was
forbidden to reveal unto mortals. "Seal up those things which
the seven thunders uttered, and write them not."‡ With the
best reason, then, is the formula inscribed on a talisman of
the first class, for hear what the *Pistis-Sophia* delivers touching
its potency.§ "After these things his disciples said again unto
him, Rabbi, reveal unto us the mysteries of the Light of thy
Father, forasmuch as we have heard thee saying that there is
another baptism of smoke, and another baptism of the Spirit of
Holy Light, and moreover an unction of the Spirit, all which
shall bring our souls into the treasurehouse of Light. Declare
therefore unto us the mysteries of these things, so that we also
may inherit the kingdom of thy Father. Jesus said unto them,
Do ye seek after these mysteries? No mystery is more excellent

---

* This is in fact a very correct
representation, if we give each vowel
its true Greek sound, of the Hebrew
pronunciation of the word Jehovah.

† Hippolytus, vi. 48.
‡ Rev. x. 4.
§ Pistis-Sophia, cap. 378.

than they; which shall bring your souls unto the Light of Lights, unto the place of Truth and Goodness, unto the place of the Holy of holies, unto the place where is neither male nor female, neither form in that place but Light, everlasting, not to be uttered. Nothing therefore is more excellent than the mysteries which ye seek after, saving only the *mystery of the Seven Vowels and their forty and nine Powers*, and the numbers thereof. And no name is more excellent than all these (Vowels),* a Name wherein be contained all Names and all Lights and all Powers. Knowing therefore this Name, if a man shall have departed out of this body of Matter, no smoke (of the bottomless pit), neither any darkness, nor Ruler of the Sphere of Fate,† nor Angel, nor Power, shall be able to hold back the soul that knoweth that Name. But and if, after he shall have departed out of this world, he shall utter that Name unto the fire, it shall be quenched, and the darkness shall flee away. And if he shall utter that Name unto the devils of the Outer Darkness, and to the Powers thereof, they shall all faint away, and their flame shall blaze up, so that they shall cry aloud 'Thou art holy, thou art holy, O Holy One of all holies!' And if he shall utter that Name unto the Takers-away for condemnation, and their Authorities, and all their Powers, nay, even unto Barbelo,‡ and the Invisible God, and the three Triple-powered Gods, so soon as he shall have uttered that Name in those places, they shall all be shaken and thrown one upon the other, so that they shall be ready to melt away and perish, and shall cry aloud, 'O Light of all lights that art in the Boundless Light! remember us also, and purify us!'" After such a revelation as this, we need seek no further for the reason of the frequent occurrence of this formula upon talismans intended, when they had done their duty in this world, to accompany their owner into the tomb, continuing to exert there a protective influence of a yet higher order than in life.

For the student of the mineralogy of the ancients this celt

* Evidently alluding to the collocation of the vowels on our talisman.

† The twelve Æons of the Zodiac, the creators of the human soul, which they eagerly seek to catch when released from the body in which they have imprisoned it.

‡ The divine mother of the Saviour, and one of the three "Invisible Gods," cap. 359.

has very great interest in point of *material*, as being the only specimen of true jade, bearing indisputable marks of either Greek or Roman workmanship, that, so far as my knowledge extends, has ever yet been brought to light. This ancient neglect of the material is truly difficult to explain, if the statement of a very good authority, Corsi, be indeed correct, that the sort showing the deepest green is found in Egypt. The known predilection of the Romans for gems of that colour, would, one should naturally expect, have led them in that case to employ the stone largely in ornamentation, after the constant fashion of the Chinese, and to value it as a harder species of the *Smaragdus*. The circumstances under which this relic was brought to England render it more than probable that Egypt was the place where it was found; a supposition corroborated by the fine quality of the stone exactly agreeing with what Corsi remarks of the Egyptian kind. That *Alexandria* was the place where the inscription was added upon its surface can admit of little question; the lettering being precisely that seen upon innumerable other monuments which can with certainty be assigned to the same grand focus of Gnosticism. In addition to this, it is very doubtful whether in the third or fourth centuries a lapidary could have been found elsewhere throughout the whole Roman Empire capable of engraving with such skill as the minute characters within the wreath evince, upon a material of this, almost insuperable, obduracy. From the times of the Ptolemies down to the Arab conquest, and even later, Alexandria was the seat of the manufacture of vases in rock crystal. This trade served to keep alive the expiring Glyptic art for the only purpose for which its productions continued to be demanded—the manufacture of talismans, consignments of which must have been regularly shipped, together with the crystal-ware,* to Rome, and equally to the other important cities of the empire.

The primitive Egyptians, like the early Chaldeans, used stone in the place of metal for their cutting instruments, and continued its use for making particular articles down into historic times. Herodotus mentions the regular employment of

* " Dum tibi Niliacus portat crystalla cataplus."—Mart. xii. 72.

the "Ethiopian stone" sharpened, for a dissecting-knife* in the process of embalming, and similarly for pointing the arrows† carried by the contingent of the same nation in the army of Xerxes. The Alexandrian citizen, half-Jew half-Greek, who had the good fortune to pick up this primæval implement, doubtless rejoiced in the belief that he had gotten a "stone of virtue," most potent alike from substance, figure, and nature, and therefore proceeded to do his prize due honour by making it the *medium* of his most accredited spells—nay, more, by inventing a new formula of unusual complication and profundity whereby to animate its inherent powers. As regards its *substance*, the stone probably passed then for a *smaragdus* of exceptional magnitude, and that gem, as Pliny records,‡ was recommended by the magi as the proper material for a talisman of prodigious efficacy, which, duly engraved, should baffle witchcraft, give success at court, avert hailstorms, and much more of like nature. The *smaragdus* of the ancients was little more than a generic designation for all stones of a *green* colour, and the entire Gnostic series strikingly demonstrates that this hue was deemed a primary requisite in a talismanic gem—the almost exclusive material of the class being the green jasper and the plasma.

Again, as regards *figure*, this celt offered in its *triangular* outline, that most sacred of all emblems, the mystic Delta, the form that signified maternity, and was the hieroglyph of the moon. This belief is mentioned by Plutarch,§ and explains why the triangle so often accompanies the figure of the sacred baboon, Luna's special attribute, on monuments, where also it is sometimes displayed elevated upon a column with that animal standing before it in the attitude of adoration.

Lastly, the supposed *nature* of this gift of Fortune was not of Earth, inasmuch as it then passed for a holy thing that "had fallen down from Jupiter," being, in fact, nothing less than one of that god's own thunderbolts. A notion this which will

* ii. 86.
† vii. 69.
‡ xxxvii. 40.
§ 'De Iside et Osiride,' cap. 75. He adds that the Pythagoreans called the equilateral triangle "Athene"—a curious confirmation of the tradition quoted by Aristotle, that the Attic goddess was one and the same with the Moon.

doubtless strike the modern mind as so strange, or rather as so
preposterous, that it necessitates my giving at full length my
reasons for making such an assertion. And in truth the subject
is well worth the trouble of investigation, seeing that the same
superstition will be found to extend from an early period of
antiquity down into the popular belief of our own times
throughout a large extent of Europe.

It is in accordance with this notion that I have designated
this celt a "ceraunia" (thunderbolt-stone), and it therefore
remains for me to adduce my reasons for giving it what must
appear to most people so unaccountable and highly inappro-
priate an appellation. *Sotacus*, who is quoted elsewhere by
Pliny "as one of the most ancient writers on mineralogy," is
cited by him* "as making two other kinds of the ceraunia, the
black and the red, resembling *axe-heads* in shape. Of these,
such as be black and round are sacred things; towns and fleets
can be captured by their instrumentality. The latter are called
Bætyli, whilst the oblong sort are the *Cerauniæ.* Some make
out another kind, in mighty request in the practices of the
magi, inasmuch as it is only to be found in places that have
been struck by lightning." One would have been utterly at a
loss to understand what the old Greek had been speaking about
in the chapter thus confusedly condensed by the later Roman
naturalist, or to discover any resemblance in form between the
lightning-flash and an axe-head, had it not been for the popular
superstition that has prevailed in Germany from time immemorial to the present day, and of which full particulars are
given by Anselmus Boëtius in his invaluable repertory of
mediæval lore upon all such matters, written at the beginning
of the seventeenth century.†

Under the popular names of "Strahl-hammer," "Donner-
pfeil," "Donner-keil," "Strahl-pfeil," "Strahl-keil" (lightning-
hammer, thunder-arrow or club, lightning-arrow, &c.), and the
Italian "Sagitta,"‡ he figures stone celts and hammers of five

different, but all common, types; remarking that so firm was the belief in these things being the "actual arrow of the lightning" (ipsa fulminis sagitta), that should any one attempt to controvert it he would be taken for a madman. He however confesses with amusing simplicity that the substance of these thunderbolts is exceedingly like the common flint used for striking fire with; nay, more, he boldly declares he should agree with those few *rationalists* who, on the strength of their resemblance in shape to the tools in common use, pronounced these objects to be merely ordinary iron implements that had got *petrified* by long continuance in the earth, had it not been for the testimony of the most respectable witnesses as to the fact of their being discovered in places just seen to be struck with lightning. Besides quoting some fully detailed instances from Gesner, he adds that several persons had assured him of having themselves seen these stones dug up in places where the lightning had fallen. The natural philosophers of the day accounted for the creation of such substances in the atmosphere by supposing the existence of a vapour charged with sulphureous and metallic particles, which rising above a certain height became condensed through the extreme heat of the sun, and assumed a wedge-like form in consequence of the escape of their moisture, and the gravitation of the heavier particles towards their lower end! Notwithstanding this celestial origin, the virtue of the production was not then esteemed of a proportionally sublime order, extending no further than to the prevention or the cure of ruptures in children, if placed upon their cradles; and also to the procuring of sleep in the case of adults. In our own times Justinus Kerner mentions* the same names for stone celts as universally popular amongst the German boors; but they are now chiefly valued for their efficacy in preserving cattle from the murrain, and consequently the finders can seldom be induced to part with them.

---

not of this world,—using those of the *lingua militaris* for every-day purposes. The flint arrow-heads found in the *terra marna* of the primæval Umbrian towns, are believed by the peasantry to have this celestial origin, and are highly valued as portable "light-conductors."

* In his little treatise on Amulets.

It must not, however, be supposed that Sotacus picked up
this strange notion from the Teutones of his own age, whose
very existence was probably unknown to him; his informants
were unquestionably those magi cited at the conclusion of
Pliny's extract.   The Greek mineralogist had lived " apud
Regem," that is, at the court of the King of Persia, very probably in the capacity of royal physician, like his countrymen
Democedes and Ctesias.   In that region he had ample oppor-
tunities of seeing stone celts, for Rawlinson observes * that
flint axes and other implements, exactly identical with the
European in workmanship, are *common* in all the most ancient
mounds of Chaldæa, those sites of primæval cities.   Such
elevations above the dead level of those interminable plains
were necessarily the most liable to be lightning-struck; and
hence probably arose the idea that these weird-looking stones
(all tradition of whose proper destination had long since died
out amongst the iron-using Persians) were the actual fiery bolts
which had been seen to bury themselves in the clay.   And
again, to revert to the German belief, it must be remembered
that Thor, the Northern Jupiter, is pictured as armed with a
huge hammer in the place of the classical thunderbolt.   The
type of the god had been conceived in the far-remote ages when
the stone-hammer was as yet the most effective and formidable
of weapons, and was preserved unchanged out of deference to
antiquity, after the true meaning of the attribute was entirely
forgotten.   Nevertheless, his worshippers, accustomed to behold the hammer in the hand of the god of thunder,—ὑψιβρεμέτης
Ζεύς,—very naturally concluded that these strange objects, of
unknown use, found from time to time deep buried in the
earth, were the actual missiles which that deity had discharged.
It is a remarkable proof of the wide diffusion of the same belief,
that the late owner of the relic under consideration, habitually
spoke of it as a " thunderstone,"—a name he could only have
learnt from the Arabs from whom it was procured, seeing that
no such notion with respect to *celts* has ever been current in
this country.   But every one whose memory reaches back forty
years or more may recollect, that wheresoever in England the

* 'Ancient Monarchies,' i. p. 120.

fossil *Belemnite* is to be found, it was implicitly received by all, except the few pioneers of Geology (a word then almost synonymous with Atheism), as the veritable thunderbolt shot from the clouds, and by that appellation was it universally known. I, for one, can recollect stories, quite as respectably attested as those Boëtius quotes concerning the *Cerauniæ*, told respecting the discovery of new fallen belemnites under precisely the same circumstances; and, in truth, the same author does in the preceding chapter treat at length of the *Belemnites*, and his cuts show that the name meant then what it does at present; but he assigns to the missile an infernal instead of a celestial source, giving the vulgar title for it as "Alpschoss," (elfin-shot,) which he classically renders into "dart of the Incubus," stating further that it was esteemed (on the good old principle, "similia similibus curantur") of mighty efficacy to guard the sleeper from the visits of that much dreaded nocturnal demon. The Prussian, Saxon, and Spanish physicians employed it, powdered, as equally efficacious with the *lapis Judaicus*, in the treatment of the calculus. It was also believed a specific for the pleurisy in virtue of its *pointed* figure, which was analogous to the *sharp* pains of that disease, for so taught the universally accepted "Doctrine of Signatures."

The *Ceraunia* of Sotacus, however, comprised, besides these primitive manufactures of man, other substances, it is hard to say whether meteorites or fossils; the nature of which remains to be discussed. Photius,[*] after quoting the paragraph, "I beheld the *Bætylus* moving through the air, and sometimes wrapped up in vestments, sometimes carried in the hands of the ministers," proceeds to give a summary of the wondrous tale told by the discoverer of the prodigy—one Eusebius of Emesa. He related how that, being seized one night with a sudden and unaccountable desire to visit a very ancient temple of Minerva, situated upon a mountain at some distance from the city, he started off, and arriving at the foot, sat down to rest himself. Suddenly he beheld a globe of fire fall down from heaven, and a monstrous lion standing by the same, but who

[*] 'Bibliotheca,' 1063, R.

immediately vanished. Running to pick it up as soon as the fire was extinguished, he found this self-same *Bætylus*. Inquiring of it to what god it belonged, the thing made answer that he came from the Noble One (so was called a figure of a lion standing in the temple at Heliopolis). Eusebius thereupon ran home with his prize, a distance of 210 stadia (26 miles), without once stopping, being quite unable to control the *impetus* of the stone! He described it as "of a whitish colour, a perfect sphere, a span in diameter, but sometimes assuming a purple* shade, and also expanding and contracting its dimensions, and having letters painted on it in cinnabar, of which he gave the interpretation. The stone, likewise, if struck against the wall, returned answers to consultors in a low whistling voice." The grain of truth in this huge heap of lies is obviously enough the fact that Eusebius, having had the good fortune to witness the descent of a meteorite, and to get possession of the same, told all these fables about it in order to increase the credit of the oracular stone (which doubtless brought him in many fees) amongst his credulous townsfolk. Damascius† (whose Life of Isidorus Photius is here being epitomised) adds, that this philosopher was of opinion that the stone was the abode of a spirit, though not one of the mischievous or unclean sort, nor yet one of a perfectly immaterial nature. He furthermore states that other *bætyli* were known, dedicated to Saturn, Jupiter, and the Sun; and moreover that Isidorus and himself saw many of such *bætyli* or *bætylia* upon Mount Libanus, near Heliopolis in Syria.

As for the derivation of *bætylus*, the one proposed by the Byzantine Hesychius, who makes it come from *bæte*, the goatskin mantle, wherein Rhea wrapped up the stone she gave old Saturn to swallow, instead of the new-born Jove, cannot be considered much more satisfactory than Bochart's, who, like a sound divine, discovers in it a reminiscence of the stone pillar which Jacob set up at Bethel, and piously endeavours to force Sanconiathon, who speaks of the "living" stones, the bæthylia,‡

* The Greek purple included every shade from crimson to violet.

† A stoic philosopher under Justinian.

‡ "Moreover the god Uranus devised *bæthylia*, contriving stones that moved as having life."

to confirm his interpretation by correcting his text into "anointed."

But this last *bætylus* is beyond all question the same thing with that described by the Pseudo-Orpheus,* under the names of *Siderites*, and the *animated Orites*, " round, black, ponderous, and surrounded with deeply-graven furrows." In the first of these epithets may easily be recognized the *ferruginous* character common to all meteorites (*siderites* being also applied to the loadstone), whilst the second (*Orites*) seems to indicate the locality where they most abounded, viz., Mount Lebanon.

Sotacus' notice, indeed, of the efficacy of the *bætylus* in procuring success in seafights and sieges, is copiously illustrated by the succeeding verses of the same mystic poet, who, it must be remembered, can claim a very high antiquity, there being sufficient grounds for identifying him with Onomacritus, a contemporary of Pisistratus, in the sixth century before our era. The diviner Helenus, according to him, had received this oracular stone from Apollo, and he describes the rites, with great minuteness, for the guidance of all subsequent possessors of such a treasure, by means of which the Trojan woke up the spirit within the " vocal sphere." This was effected by dint of thrice seven days' fasting and continence, by incantations and sacrifices offered to the stone, and by bathing, clothing, and nursing it like an infant. Through its aid, when at length rendered instinct with life, the traitorous seer declared to the Atridæ the coming downfall of Troy; the stone uttering its responses in a voice resembling the feeble wail of an infant desiring the breast. It is more than probable that Orphesius in describing the Orites, had in view the *Sālagrāma*, or sacred stone of Vishnu, still employed by the Brahmins in all propitiatory rites, especially in those performed at the death-bed. Sonnerat describes it as " a kind of ammonite, round or oval in shape, black, and very ponderous." The *furrows* covering its surface were traced by Vishnu's own finger ; but when found of a violet colour, it is looked upon with horror, as representing a vindictive avatār of the god. The possessor keeps it wrapped up in linen garment like a child, and often bathes

* Λιθικά, 355.

P

and perfumes it—precisely the rites prescribed by our poet for
the due consultation of the oracle of the Siderites.

From all this it may safely be deduced that the " stone of
power," whether *bætylus* or *orites,* was in most cases nothing
more than a fossil; either a ferruginous nodule, or an echinus
filled with iron pyrites.   Their being found in abundance in one
particular locality, precludes the idea of these at least being
meteorites, which latter, besides, never assume any regular form,
but look like mere fragments of iron slag.   This explanation is
strongly supported by the drawings Boetius gives* of what was
then called the " Donner-stein," or " Wetter-stein," (thunder, or
storm-stone,) and which he very plausibly identifies with
Pliny's *Brontias* " that got into the head of the tortoise during
thunder-storms," and which is described in another place as
the " eye of the Indian tortoise " that conferred the gift of
prophecy.   His carefully drawn figure of this Donner-stein
(which also passed for the " grosser Kroten-stein," bigger toadstone), shows it to be only a fossil echinus of a more *oblate* form
than the common sort.   The regular toadstone, plentifully to be
seen in mediæval rings, was, on the other hand, the small
hollow hemisphere, the fossil tooth of an extinct fish, found in
the greensand formation.   In that age the Donner-stein was
held to possess all the many virtues of the Toadstone, Belemnite, and Ovum Anguinum, in counteracting poison, giving
success in all enterprises, procuring sleep, and protection
against danger of lightning.   But the old physician, so much
in advance of his times, cannot help winding up the list of its
virtues with the hint, " Fides sæpe veritate major."

The axe-heads and hammer-heads of stone, known to us by
the general designation of celts, have, until recent explorations,
been regarded as comparatively of rare occurrence amongst
ancient relics obtained from Eastern lands and from some other
continental countries.   Our information, however, in regard
to objects of this class has become greatly extended.   Mr.
James Yates published, in the Archæological Journal, examples of stone celts from Java ; an interesting specimen
obtained at Sardis is figured, vol. xv. p. 178, and some others

* ii. cap. 264.

were found by Mr. Layard at Nineveh. The occurrence of any ornament or inscription upon such objects is very rare, but amongst numerous stone implements obtained in Greece one is noticed by M. de Mortillet (Matériaux pour l'Histoire primitive de l'Homme, Jan. 1868, p. 9), of which he had received from Athens a drawing and an *estampage*; it is described as "une hache en pierre serpentineuse, sur une des faces de laquelle on a gravé trois personnages et une inscription en caractères grecs. L'ancien outil a évidemment été, beaucoup plus tard, quand on a eu complétement oublié son usage primitif, transformé en talisman ou pierre cabalistique."

At the annual meeting of the Antiquaries of the North, on March 21st, 1853, under the presidency of the late King of Denmark, several recent acquisitions were exhibited, obtained for his private collection at Frederiksborg. Amongst these there was an axe-head of stone (length about 6½ inches), perforated with a hole for the handle, and remarkable as bearing on one of its sides four Runic characters, that appear to have been cut upon the stone at some period more recent than the original use of the implement. It has been figured in the Memoirs of the Society, 1850–1860, p. 28 ; see also Antiquarisk Tidsskrift, 1852-1854, pp. 258–266. I am indebted to a friend well skilled in Runes and Scandinavian archæology, Dr. Charlton, formerly secretary of the Society of Antiquaries of Newcastle, for the following observations on this interesting relic.

"The first letter is L, and, if we accept the idea that these were Runes of Victory, it may stand for the initial of Loki; the second is Th, and may stand for Thor; the third O for Odin ; the fourth, Belgthor, with a T above it, may refer to Belgthor's friendship and alliance with Thor, and the T stands for Tyr. We may imagine the names of the Northern gods to have been cut on this stone axe to give it victory in battle, just as the old Germans and Saxons cut mystic Runes on their swords, a practice noticed by Haigh in his 'Conquest of Britain by the Saxons,' p. 28, pl. 1, where he has figured amongst various examples of the *futhorc*, or alphabet of Runic characters, one inlaid on a sword or knife found in the Thames, and now in the British Museum. At p. 51, *ibid.* pl. iii. fig. 20, he has cited also the Runic inscription on the silver pommel of a sword found at Gilton, Kent, formerly in the collection of the late Mr. Rolfe, of Sandwich, and subsequently in the possession of Mr. Joseph Mayer. This relic is now in the precious museum bestowed by his generous encouragement of archæological science on the town of Liverpool. The interpretation given in the latter instance is as follows,—I eke victory to great deeds.*

"There was another explanation given of the characters on the Danish stone axe. It was read—LUTHER. o.—Ludr owns namely, the weapon thus inscribed."

In the ancient Sagas, as remarked in Nilsson's ' Primitive Inhabitants of Scandinavia ' (translation by Sir John Lubbock, Bart, p. 214), mention occurs of amulets designated life-stones. victory-stones, &c., which warriors carried about with them in battle to secure victory. A curious relation is cited from one of the Sagas, that King Nidung, when about to engage in conflict, perceived that he had neglected to bring a precious heir-loom, a stone that possessed the virtue of ensuring victory. He offered the hand of his daughter, with a third part of his kingdom, to him who should bring this talisman before the fight commenced ; and, having received it, he won the battle. In another narrative, the daughter of a Scanian warrior steals during his slumbers the stone that was hung on his neck, and gave it to her lover, who thus became the victor. Nilsson observes that stones are found in museums, for instance a hammer-stone with a loop, that appear to have been worn thus as talismans in war.

It is perhaps scarcely necessary to advert to certain axe-heads of stone, in their general form similar to those with which we are familiar as found in Europe ; upon these implements are engraved rude designs, such as the human visage, &c. These objects, of which an example preserved in a museum at Douai has been much cited, may be " victory-stones " of an ancient and primitive people, but they are now recognised as of Carib origin, and not European.

* ' Archæologia,' vol. xxxii. p. 321. A spear-head inscribed with Runes is noticed, ' Journ. Brit. Arch. Ass.,' vol. xxiii. p. 387. There exist certain massive rings of metal inscribed with Runes, that may have been, as some antiquaries suggest, appended to sword-hilts as charms. One of these rings, lately found at Carlisle, is in possession of Mr. Robert Ferguson, of Morton, near that city.

CPSIA information can be obtained at www.ICGtesting.com
Printed in the USA
LVOW021407081211

258467LV00001B/1/A